the 50

GREATEST CASTLES AND PALACES
OF THE WORLD

IN ASSOCIATION WITH
TIMPSON

the 50

GREATEST CASTLES AND PALACES

OF THE WORLD

GILLY PICKUP

Published in the UK in 2019 by
Icon Books Ltd, Omnibus Business Centre,
39–41 North Road, London N7 9DP
email: info@iconbooks.com
www.iconbooks.com

Sold in the UK, Europe and Asia
by Faber & Faber Ltd, Bloomsbury House,
74–77 Great Russell Street,
London WC1B 3DA or their agents

Distributed in the UK, Europe and Asia
by Grantham Book Services, Trent Road,
Grantham NG31 7XQ

Distributed in Australia and New Zealand
by Allen & Unwin Pty Ltd,
PO Box 8500, 83 Alexander Street,
Crows Nest, NSW 2065

Distributed in South Africa by
Jonathan Ball, Office B4, The District,
41 Sir Lowry Road, Woodstock 7925

Distributed in India by Penguin Books India,
7th Floor, Infinity Tower – C, DLF Cyber City,
Gurgaon 122002, Haryana

Distributed in Canada by Publishers Group Canada,
76 Stafford Street, Unit 300, Toronto, Ontario M6J 2S1

Distributed in the USA by Publishers Group West,
1700 Fourth Street, Berkeley, CA 94710

ISBN: 978-178578-457-6

Images – see individual pictures

Typeset and designed by Simmons Pugh

Printed and bound in Great Britain by Clays Ltd, Elcograf S.p.A.

Love and thanks to Mike for the never-ending supply of encouragement and input.

Sweet memories of my mum.

ABOUT THE AUTHOR

Gilly Pickup is an award-winning journalist specialising in travel and cruise but also publishing features on the arts, history, wellbeing, animals, food, alternative health, heritage, gardens and the supernatural. Her bylines appear in national newspapers, newsstand magazines, specialist and trade titles and inflight publications. She is also the sole author of nine books.

Before becoming a writer, she worked in the Palace of Westminster (Houses of Parliament) as a senior political researcher.

Gilly was born and brought up in north-east Scotland and lives in London.

See more at www.gillypickup.co.uk

CONTENTS

NORTH AMERICA

Canada

United States of America

INTRODUCTION

What is the difference between a castle and a palace? Generally speaking, a castle was built for defence purposes with battlements, thick walls, arrow slits, gatehouses and moats, all designed to protect the inhabitants. A palace shows the world how powerful and wealthy the inhabitants are or were and were usually built as royal residences.

There are so many fascinating castles and palaces in the world that it is hard to choose just 50 to include in this book.

Many thrill with their flamboyancy – indeed, some look as if they have been plucked directly from the pages of a fairy tale. Take Germany's fantasy Neuschwanstein Castle for instance, home to that delightfully eccentric monarch, Ludwig II. Then there's Picardy's Château de Pierrefonds, a blend of Gothic and romantic Renaissance styles. This multi-level turreted showstopper has starred in several swashbuckling French films including *The Messenger: Story of Joan of Arc*. It stood in for Camelot in the BBC series *Merlin* too.

Others are forbidding places, harbouring all manner of dark secrets and, naturally, a ghost or two. Seriously spooky 13th-century Chillingham Castle in Northumberland falls into this category with one of the highest levels of paranormal activity in Britain. Countless spectres and apparitions have been recorded by visitors over the years and regular ghost tours are held for those who dare to be scared. If you're really brave, you can stay for an all-night vigil. Another creepy fortress is the intriguing 14th-century Bran Castle, perched high among craggy peaks in Romania's Carpathian Mountains. Often referred to as 'Dracula's Castle' because it closely fits Bram Stoker's description, it is actually one of several castles linked to the legend.

Some are still royal residences including India's grey granite and pink marble Mysore Palace, official residence of the Wadiyar dynasty. Other royal residences include the Royal Palace of Brussels and Madrid's Palacio Real, though these days both families prefer to live their daily lives in more modest surroundings.

Others are as big as, well, entire towns. Take for instance the Forbidden City (Old Palace) in Beijing, home to China's emperors from the Ming dynasty to the end of the Qing dynasty. Comprising around 1,000 buildings, up to 1 million workers were involved in its construction. Occupying an area of 700,000 square metres, Topkapi Palace in Turkey is another supersize structure as is Poland's UNESCO-listed Malbork Castle, Europe's largest Gothic pile.

I have included one of my personal favourites, Glamis Castle, located a few miles from where I was born and brought up in the county of Angus in Scotland. It is almost Disneyesque in appearance with witch-hat turrets and links to *Macbeth*. It was the birthplace of the late Queen Mother and historic seat of her family, the Bowes-Lyons. Still in Scotland, Edinburgh Castle, Scotland's number one visitor attraction is perched on an extinct volcano. This powerful national symbol is home to the Scottish Crown Jewels. Speaking of Crown Jewels, the Tower of London, royal palace and secure fortress, has served as an armoury, treasury, menagerie and home of the Royal Mint. It simply drips with history.

Let me say that if I have missed out your particular favourite palace or castle, then my apologies. There are so many worthy contenders out there that I would need to write another book to include all of them! The ones I chose to write about either have a fascinating story to tell or make a great day out. Or indeed both.

UNITED KINGDOM

– ENGLAND –

ALNWICK CASTLE, NORTHUMBERLAND

If you think you recognise this magnificent pile as Hogwarts from the Harry Potter films, you'd be right. Alnwick Castle is the second-largest inhabited castle in England. Windsor Castle is the first, in case you're wondering.

Home to the Percys, the Dukes of Northumberland, the castle dates back to around 1100 when a castle was founded by de Vesci, a nobleman from Normandy. His daughter married Eustace Fitz John who became Baron of Alnwick. Eustace saw to it that the castle's fortifications were impregnable and it survived an attack by William the Lion, King of Scotland in 1172. Not that William gave up, he tried again a couple of years later but, bad luck – the English captured him and later he signed a treaty acknowledging fealty to King Henry II to regain his freedom. However, that was rescinded in 1189 by King Richard I for 10,000 silver marks, to pay for Richard's participation in the third crusade.

The castle has witnessed several new brooms – perhaps apt considering its connection to Harry Potter – having a series of owners, and was purchased in 1309 from the Bishop of Durham by wealthy Henry Percy. Henry and his son spent

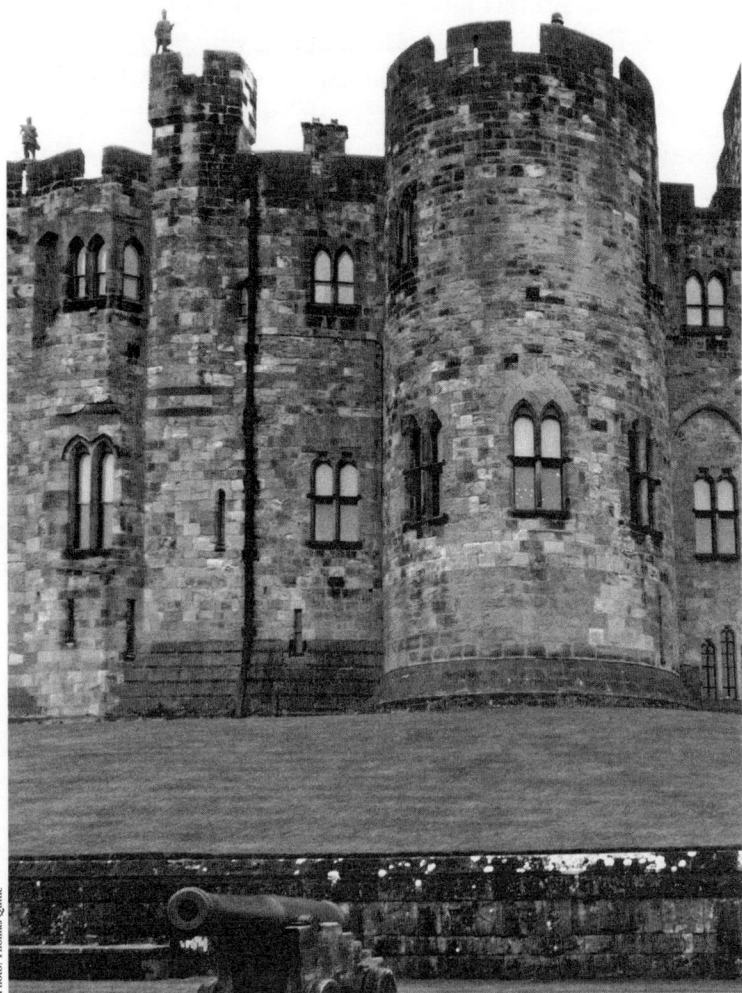

Photo: Thomas Quine

years developing the castle and made it a significant fortress, an important military post against Scottish and border reivers – that is those people who raided and stole goods in the area where Scotland meets England. Things were so fraught between the two countries that in 1433 King Henry VI granted a licence to the town of Alnwick to be enclosed in a wall to help protect it from attack by the Scots.

In the 17th century the castle fell into disrepair but in the mid-18th century architects Daniel Garrett, James Paine and Robert Adam set about transforming it and the grounds. In the mid-19th century the castle was done up again, with the exterior reflecting its medieval origins.

Over the years Alnwick has served as a military outpost, a teaching college, a refuge for evacuees and of course as a family home. One of its most glamorous functions is as a film set. It first appeared in *Prince Valiant* in 1954, and there have been twelve more productions featuring the site since then. After all, it does have a dramatic appearance. It has appeared in television programmes *Downton Abbey* (2014 and 2015) and *Blackadder* (1983), and had star appearances in *Robin Hood: Prince of Thieves* (1991), *Harry Potter and the Chamber of Secrets* (2002) and *Harry Potter and the Philosopher's Stone* (2001).

Following in Harry's footsteps it was felt it would be a good idea to introduce broomstick flying training for visitors from the resident wizards. And for those who decide to have a go, they can take home photos of their successful flight, to show other muggles. Lessons are as popular with adults as they are with kids and take place several times a day, but ideally should be booked online in advance. The castle holds special events throughout the year and it's probably no surprise that one of these is Wizard Week, where visitors can enjoy all sorts of spell-binding sorcery and visit locations where scenes from the Harry Potter films were shot.

Coming back down to earth, visitors can see the magnificent richly-decorated State Rooms with ceilings inspired by the Vatican and Castle St Angelo in Rome. There are two baroque cabinets which were made especially for the Palace of Versailles and an explosion of paintings with works by Titian, Canaletto and Van Dyke. A library of 15,000 books is said to be the family's favourite room. The see-and-be-seen drawing room has a painted and gilded ceiling, silk wall hangings and a huge mirror above an ornate marble fireplace. Besides all that, the castle has a prestigious display of Meissen and Chelsea ceramics.

When you've had enough of the serious side of visiting, you can have a bit of fun in the artisan's courtyard, a representation of life in the 14th century. There you can dress up and create your own family fairy tale.

There are three museums in the castle. One is the Museum of the Northumberland Fusiliers, not just an educational museum but hands-on too. There is another dressing-up room here where visitors can try on various uniforms. The Castle Museum was founded in 1826 by the 4th Duke of Northumberland and the Constable's Tower, re-opened in 2018, has three floors of exhibits including items collected by various dukes from far flung places including America and Polynesia. One area is devoted to the Percy Tenantry Volunteers, a regiment set up at the end of the 18th century during the Napoleonic Wars. It displays lots of weaponry.

The grounds of the castle are worth seeing too. Much of the area was designed by Capability Brown and more recently Jane Percy, the present Duchess, founded the Alnwick Garden. Inspired by the Medici poison garden in Italy, the Duchess also opened a Poison Garden in 2005. It is full to the brim with some seriously deadly poisonous and hallucinogenic plants, many of which have to be kept under lock and key. There is hemlock, deadly nightshade, digitalis, foxglove, mandrake, ricin and strychnine and what's more, a copper snake sprays mist into the air to add a sense of mystery. And would you believe, despite being warned not to touch or smell the plants, it is not unheard of to find visitors who have ignored the warnings lying unconscious in the garden.

Interesting facts about Alnwick Castle:

• Famous warrior Harry Hotspur was born at Alnwick Castle around 1365, and was the son of the 1st Earl of Northumberland.

• Algernon Percy, 4th Duke (1792–1865) was only twelve years old when he joined the navy.

• One of the world's largest wooden tree houses is in the garden and functions as a restaurant. It comes with wooden walkways and wobbly rope bridges.

Address: Alnwick Castle, Greenwell Lane, Alnwick, NE66 1NQ

Website: https://www.alnwickcastle.com

Visitor information: The castle is open daily between the end of March and October. Although there are around 150 rooms in the castle, only six of them are open to the public, including the lavish State Rooms, Drawing Room, Dining Room, and Library. Regular events take place in the castle and gardens, see website for details.

BLENHEIM PALACE, OXFORDSHIRE

Home to the 12th Duke of Marlborough and birthplace of Sir Winston Churchill, Blenheim Palace is a UNESCO World Heritage Site and the only non-royal, non-episcopal English country house to hold the title of palace.

Blenheim Palace was originally Woodstock Manor, a royal hunting lodge. Princess Elizabeth (later Queen Elizabeth I) was once imprisoned here for her alleged role in the Wyatt plot, which aimed to prevent Queen Mary's marriage to King Philip of Spain.

The manor house and grounds were given to John Churchill, 1st Duke of Marlborough, as a gift from Queen Anne and a grateful nation. A nice present to honour his victory as the military commander who led allied forces in the battle of Blenheim in the War of the Spanish Succession on 13 August 1704. Although the manor was in ruins, he was also granted the sum of £240,000 so that he could have a house built to commemorate what he had achieved.

The Duke's wife Sarah was a close friend of Queen Anne's and became her Lady of the Bedchamber. Indeed it is suggested that there was a passion between the two women that went far beyond mere friendship. Anne's father did not approve of the appointment, perhaps fearing that Sarah would dominate his daughter. Before long, lovesick Anne was at Sarah's beck and call. Letters from Anne to Sarah show the extent of her feelings: 'If I writ whole volumes I could never express how well I love you,' she gushed. The formidable Sarah later wrote that Anne 'desired to possess [me] wholly'. However, in those days attitudes to friendship

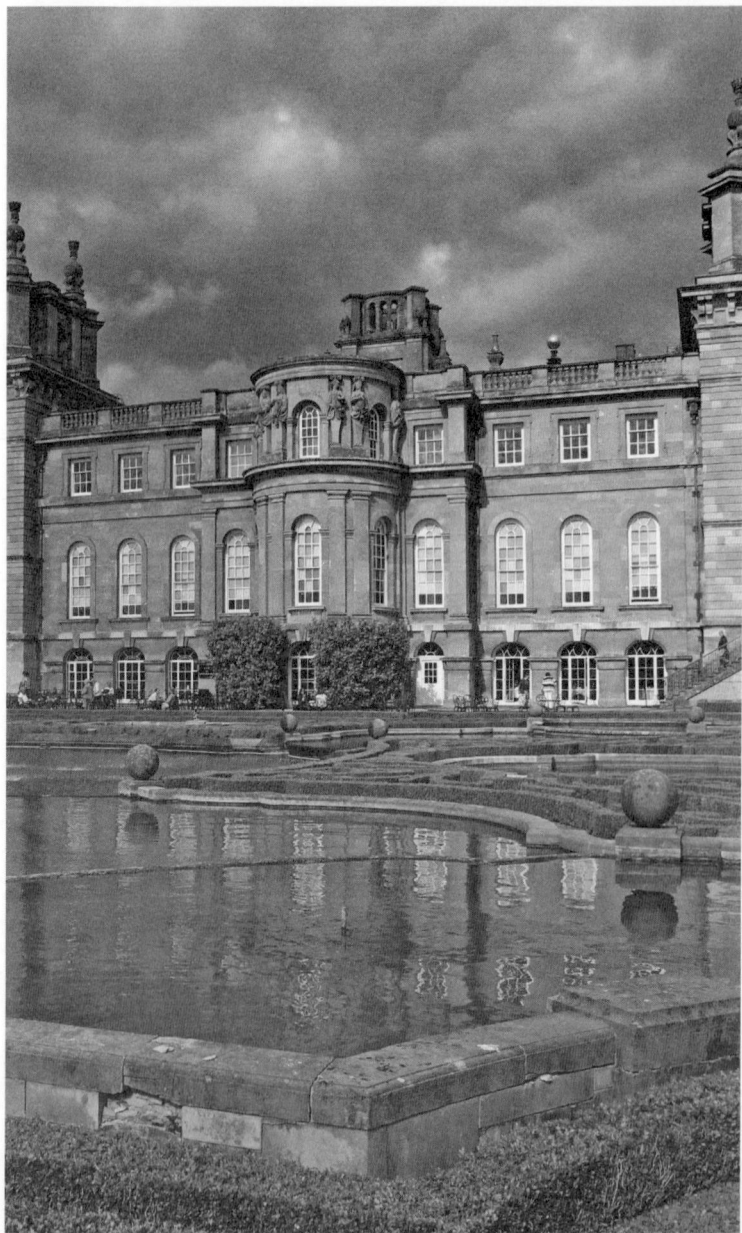

Photo: Bjoern Eisbaer

and love were different than they are today, so although one can surmise, no one can actually be 100 per cent certain of the true nature of their relationship. It wasn't all plain sailing though, because Sarah had a violent temper, and on one occasion there was a quarrel between her and the queen in St Paul's Cathedral. The reason was that Sarah noticed Anne was not wearing the jewellery she had laid out for her. Sarah turned huffy and bickered with the queen inside the cathedral. Over time their arguments became more frequent, and the final straw to end the relationship was when Sarah tried to control how the queen mourned her dead husband.

During the 1800s, the family's financial woes meant the 2nd Duke of Marlborough auctioned several books, paintings and furniture to clear his debts. The family's financial situation then improved, indeed probably saving Blenheim from ruin, when during the 19th century two of the men married rich American heiresses. Jennie Jerome, daughter of a wealthy New Yorker became the wife of Lord Randolph Churchill, and then mother to Winston Churchill. In 1896 the 9th Duke of Marlborough also married a rich American, eighteen-year-old Consuelo Vanderbilt, who came on board with a dowry – and a large one at that – $2.5 million. She was a kindly person who regularly got involved with charity works and became known as the 'Angel of Woodstock'. However, unfortunately it wasn't a happy marriage, and the couple divorced. The 9th Duke remarried; his second wife was also American and a friend of Consuelo's but they also later separated.

There is a painting on view of the Marlborough Gem collection, items which were acquired by the 4th Duke in the mid-18th century. Unfortunately the gems themselves are no longer at Blenheim, since the 7th Duke sold the lot for £10,000 in 1875.

Of course, the palace's most famous occupant was Winston Churchill, grandson of the 8th Duke. He was born in a small room off the Great Hall. The birthplace was unintentional – his parents had decided the child should be born at their London home, however his premature arrival left them unprepared. His father, Randolph Churchill, described the unexpected nature of Winston's birth in a letter to his mother-in-law: 'She [Jennie] had a fall on Tuesday walking with the shooters, and a rather imprudent and rough drive in a pony carriage brought on the pains on Saturday night. We tried to stop them, but it was no use. They went on all Sunday. Of course the Oxford physician did not come. We telegraphed for the London man, Dr Hope, but he did not arrive till this morning. The country Dr is however a clever man, and the baby was safely born at 1.30 this morning after about eight hours of labour.'

Between the saloon – a state dining room used by the family once a year on Christmas Day – and the Long Library are three interconnecting areas known as the First, Second and Third State Rooms. All three rooms have the Victory Tapestries hanging on the walls. These were commissioned by the 1st Duke of Marlborough from designer de Hondt and Brussels weaver Judocus de Vos and depict battlefield scenes in intricate and often gory detail.

The magnificent Long Library was originally designed as a picture gallery, but now contains a collection of 10,000 books – an extraordinary treasure trove, largely compiled by the 9th Duke. Full-length portraits of Queen Anne, King William III and John Churchill, 1st Duke of Marlborough, hang on the walls. At one end are marble sculptures of Queen Anne and the 1st Duke. Just outside the Green Drawing Room meanwhile, a china cabinet holds Meissen porcelain which the 3rd Duke acquired in exchange for a pack of staghounds.

Surrounding the palace are over 2,000 acres of Capability Brown parkland, lakes, fountains and formal gardens. A miniature train connects the palace to the pleasure gardens, where, among a range of fun activities for children, is the Marlborough maze, butterfly house, lavender garden and various exhibitions.

Interesting facts about Blenheim Palace:

• Productions filmed here include *Harry Potter and the Order of the Phoenix* (2007), *Gulliver's Travels* (2010), *Spectre* (2015), *The BFG* (2016) and *Transformers: The Last Knight* (2017).

• The palace has 200 rooms and 1,000 windows. When it was first built, window size was decided according to the importance of the person who lived in the room. Servants had smaller windows while family members of the duke and duchess were provided with large windows.

• Blenheim Palace was turned into a convalescent home for wounded soldiers during the First World War and during the Second World War more than 400 boys were evacuated from Malvern College to the palace. For one academic year the state rooms became dormitories and classrooms. Blenheim Park and lake was used by the Home Guard in preparation for the D-Day landings.

Address: Blenheim Palace, Woodstock, Oxfordshire, OX20 1PP

Website: www.blenheimpalace.com

Visitor information: Open to the public daily with events held throughout the year. The palace continues to develop new experiences and attractions each season and hosts special exhibitions, displays of contemporary art and seasonal specialist talks.

BUCKINGHAM PALACE, LONDON

More than 50,000 people visit Buckingham Palace each year as guests of Her Majesty the Queen at banquets, lunches, dinners, receptions and garden parties.

In the 11th century, after the Norman Conquest, the site of Buckingham House was passed to Geoffrey de Mandeville, who donated it to the monks of Westminster Abbey, whose hands it stayed in until the 1500s. Previously known as Goring House and Arlington House, the 18th-century Tory politician John Sheffield, 3rd Earl of Mulgrave and Marquess of Normanby thought that it was old fashioned, and so demolished it, or most of it, to create Buckingham House, a grand London home. He named his home after himself, as he became the Duke of Buckingham in 1703. It stood where the palace is today.

Further down the line, George III bought Buckingham House in 1762 for his wife Queen Charlotte to use as a family home. It wasn't too far from St James's Palace where many court functions were held. This was why at that time Buckingham House was known as the Queen's House and fourteen of George and Charlotte's fifteen children were born there.

It wasn't until 1826 when unpopular George IV was monarch that the house became a 'palace', although he never moved in. Even though the Duke of Wellington called

George and his brothers 'the damnedest millstones about the neck of any government that may be imagined', the King generously said the Palace could be a new home for Parliament when the Palace of Westminster was destroyed by fire in 1834. The offer was declined.

Queen Victoria took up residence in July 1837 and in June 1838 was the first British sovereign to leave for a coronation from Buckingham Palace. When she married Prince Albert in 1840, the Palace's shortcomings were highlighted. One problem was a lack of nurseries, although obviously George III hadn't found it a problem – and besides that, there weren't enough bedrooms for visitors. After much deliberation, it was decided that the only thing to be done was to move the marble arch which now stands at the corner of Hyde Park and build a fourth wing, creating a quadrangle. That's the kind of thing you can do if you're a monarch.

Edward VII was the only monarch to be born and die at Buckingham Palace. One of his dogs, a terrier named Caesar, having outlived the King, walked behind His Majesty's coffin in the funeral procession. Both Prince Charles and Prince Andrew were born here and royal birth and death notices are still attached to the railings for the public to read, although they are also now announced on the royal website.

Over the years, many distinguished figures have visited Buckingham Palace, after it became the sovereign's London residence. Roll those credits for: Felix Mendelssohn, American President J.F. Kennedy, first man on the moon Neil Armstrong, Johann Strauss the Younger, Charles Dickens, Alfred Lord Tennyson, actor Laurence Olivier, Nelson Mandela and Mahatma Gandhi, who, it is recorded, wore a loin cloth and sandals to tea with King George V.

Secret tunnels under London's streets connect Buckingham Palace to the Palace of Westminster. The story goes that the Queen Mother once explored them with King George VI and while in the tunnels they came upon a man who said he was a friend of a friend who worked in the Palace. The Queen Mother is recorded as saying he was 'a Geordie' and 'most courteous'.

Like many old buildings, Buckingham Palace has the odd phantom or two, one of which is the ghost of a monk who died in the monastery's punishment cell all those centuries ago. He is said to wear heavy chains and is dressed in brown, but for some reason only appears on the terrace over the gardens to the rear of the building on Christmas Day. Another ghost reputed to haunt the palace is that of Major John Gwynne, a private secretary to King Edward VII. Fearing disgrace in an upcoming divorce case, he shot himself in his office on the first floor and has been seen and heard at various times by members of staff.

These days the palace, which is the venue for royal ceremonies, state visits and investitures, has 775 rooms, including nineteen state rooms, 52 royal and guest bedrooms, 188 staff bedrooms, 92 offices and 78 bathrooms. It also has its own post office, swimming pool, staff cafeteria, doctor's surgery and cinema. Over 800 staff members are based at the palace, including caterers, housekeepers, horticulturalists and office staff. Some more unusual jobs include that of the fendersmith, whose job it is to clean and repair the metal fenders behind the fireplaces, and because there are more than 350 clocks and watches in the palace, two full-time horological conservators wind them up every week and keep them in good order.

There is a helicopter landing area in the palace garden, as well as a lake and tennis courts and although this is in the middle of London, 30 different bird species live there with many varieties of wild flowers flourishing in the peaceful setting.

Photo: mattbuck

Interesting facts about Buckingham Palace:

• In 1914 suffragettes seeking votes for women took their campaign to Buckingham Palace and two women chained themselves to the palace railings, as the royal family were seen to be against women having the right to vote.

• A few years later Buckingham Palace was in the news again when it had nine direct bomb hits during the Second World War. PC Steve Robertson, a policeman on duty, was killed by flying debris in March 1941 when the north side of the palace was wrecked. A plaque in the garden commemorates him.

• In 1608 King James I had the idea of planting a Mulberry Garden to the north of the present palace, in an attempt to foster the cultivation of silk worms. His idea was to make money by producing silk in England. However the idea was a non-starter and the Mulberry Garden was turned into a public recreation ground.

Address: Buckingham Palace, Westminster, London SW1

Website: www.royalcollection.org.uk/visit/the-state-rooms-buckingham-palace

Visitor information: The State Rooms are open to the public from July to September and on selected dates from September to May.

CHILLINGHAM CASTLE, NORTHUMBERLAND

The 12th-century stronghold became the fully fortified Chillingham Castle in 1344 and was continuously owned by one family line, the Grey family and their descendants, the Earls of Tankerville, from the 1200s until 1932. The many commanding generals of the castle include a record eighteen Knights of the Garter.

After the death of the 7th Earl in 1931, financial problems meant the castle fell into decay. Dry rot took hold; tower roofs collapsed, burst pipes meant flooding, windows lost their glass. It was awful. Then in the 1980s it was bought by Sir Humphry Wakefield and his wife, Katharine. Katharine, daughter of the former Lady Mary Grey, is a descendant of the family who established Chillingham.

From the outside, Chillingham Castle looks rather like you might expect a medieval castle to look: massive stone walls topped with battlements overlooking the grounds. A fantastic example of medieval strength.

King James' drawing room is Chillingham's finest apartment. Famous for its Elizabethan ceiling with finely moulded pendants, its walls are hung with tapestries and floral silk, copied from an antique design at Chatsworth. When renovations were underway after Sir Humphry's purchase, an entire staircase was discovered which had been hidden inside a wall, while in an upper room, a walled-up fireplace was uncovered, containing a wonderful cache of more than 100 Tudor documents. These included papers relating to James VI of Scotland's succession to Elizabeth I. The reason they were at Chillingham was because Lord Burghley, Elizabeth's chief minister, used his godson, Ralph Grey, as a go-between.

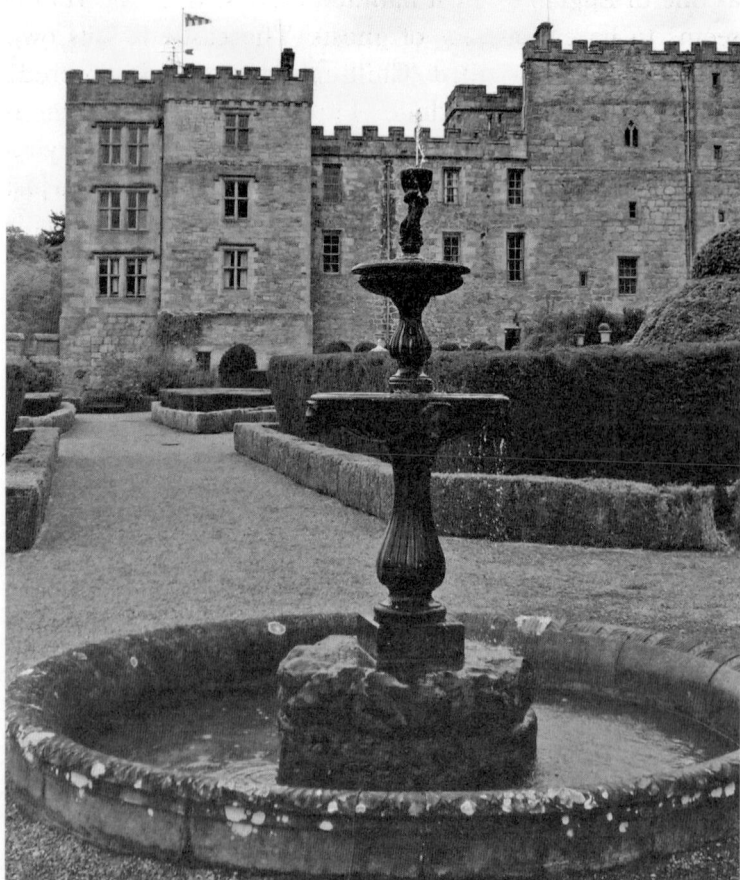

Photo: Hadrianus1959

The Edward I room is named after the so-called 'Hammer of the Scots', and he paid a visit here in 1298. King Henry III also stayed here when he came by for his Scottish forays. The room has been restored to its 13th-century format and a gallery, weapons, armour and furnishings of the time added. One wall is dominated by two huge stone fireplaces – or so it seems. The fireplaces are actually set props, brought there for the filming of *Elizabeth* starring Cate Blanchett, in 1998.

Today the castle is probably best known for its reputation as one of England's most haunted castles. Well, it certainly seems to have a surplus of ghosts. The castle has its own paranormal team called 'Chillingham Castle Uncovered'. Reports from visitors include: 'I felt this hand on my arm. It was a most friendly feeling and I believe someone was trying to guide me to see something.' Another said: 'My camera just would not take a picture of the orbs and lighting I actually saw. Yet, when I developed my film, there were those same orbs, but in different places and rooms. Literally, all over the place!' Another visitor said: 'The guide told me not to be frightened and funnily I was quite happy, even with the distinct whispering I heard in the King Edward Room.' Wow.

One spectre is called the White Pantry Ghost. Long ago, when the family silver was stored in the pantry, a footman was employed to sleep there and guard it. He said a ghost, a lady dressed in white, begged him for water. This same pale figure is still seen at times and it is thought the longing for water suggests poisoning. In the chapel, voices of two men have been heard but never seen. More famous though is the 'Radiant Boy', who used to haunt the Pink Room and whose heart rending cries of fear or pain echoed through the corridors. As the cries faded away, a bright halo of light would appear and the figure of a boy dressed in blue is known to approach those sleeping in the room, so the story goes.

Years later a child's skeleton surrounded by scraps of blue cloth was found behind the wall during repair work. After a Christian burial, the ghost was seen no more – until Sir Humphry began letting the room. Some guests have spoken of a blue flash that comes from the wall and although it has been attributed to an electrical fault, Sir Humphry explains that there is no electrical wiring in that wall section. His home seems to be full of ghosts who he said were initially hostile to him but became friendlier as restoration progressed. They even saved him from potential serious injury when he fell off a ladder, by hurling him on to bales of hay some feet away.

Another unquiet soul stalking the castle is Lady Berkeley, wife of Lord Grey, whose husband ran off with her sister, Henrietta. Lady Berkeley was left with only her baby daughter for company. The rustle of her dress is sometimes heard as her spirit sweeps along the corridors, presumably looking for her husband. A guide in the castle has encountered her several times. Spooky ...

The castle's torture chamber is not for the squeamish, packed with torture instruments including a spiked chair and a stretching rack. All manner of grisly things took place here in years gone by and I have spoken to a medium who visited. She told me that it is haunted by barbaric torturer John Sage who did his terrible deeds around AD 1200. She said that while on a visit to the castle, when the guide was telling the group about him, she heard a creaking noise, saw the heavy door open and saw a dark shadow standing by the torture rack. Isn't that scary?

Interesting facts about Chillingham Castle:

• The surrounding parkland is home to the historic Chillingham cattle, only survivors of the oldest known breed of cattle in the world. This small herd of ancient animals is a beautiful sight with their mottled white, scraggy faces, black noses and red fox-like ears. They have never been touched by human hand and no vet has ever treated one. Edward VII, once staying at the castle, thought it was fun to shoot dead the herd's king bull. Just as well that these days the only shooting visitors do is with cameras.

• Besides the cattle Chillingham Park has wildlife galore. Roe and fallow deer, brown hares, foxes and over 50 bird species including nuthatch, redstart and woodpeckers call this park home. The badgers are wary and tend to keep themselves to themselves, but ancient beech and oak trees planted around 1760 are home to the native red squirrel which you may catch sight of.

• In 1832 King Louis Philippe of France came to stay and brought with him fine urns from Versailles Palace which are still on show in the castle today.

Address: Chillingham Castle, Chillingham, Alnwick, Northumberland, NE66 5NJ

Website: www.chillingham-castle.com

Visitor information: The castle and grounds are open to the public seven months a year. Principal rooms are regularly opened to the public and licensed for weddings; one wing is reserved as private accommodation, another is divided into apartments let to holidaymakers, as is the 18th-century Coach House. Those brave folks who would like to delve deeper into Chillingham's paranormal activity can attend an all-night vigil. The castle also holds ghost tours throughout the year and if you are part of a group of ten or more, there is the option to have a candlelit meal by an open fire in the Minstrels' Hall beforehand.

CORFE CASTLE, DORSET

A survivor of the English Civil War, partially demolished in 1646 by the Parliamentarians. The name Corfe comes from an old English word meaning cutting or gap. It was one of England's first stone castles; in general, earlier castles were built with wood and earth.

The first stone of Corfe castle was laid more than 1,000 years ago and since then it has been at the centre of battles, plots and mysteries. It has had multiple uses – as a treasury, military garrison, family home and royal residence.

The castle was built during William the Conqueror's reign, for defensive purposes. The stone keep at the heart of the castle was built in the early 12th century for King Henry I, William the Conqueror's son. Let me mention here, for those not sure what a keep is, it is the most fortified part of a castle and has several floors and strong defences. The introduction of keeps allowed separate living areas for the main occupants so that they were not in close proximity to the servants, and the basement of the keep often served as a prison. The word 'keep' is the English term for the French *donjon*, which was itself taken and anglicised to form today's 'dungeon'.

King John's reign from 1199 to 1216 had its ups and downs and Corfe Castle became a refuge for this insecure monarch who had a penchant for inflicting cruelty on those who annoyed him. It was also somewhere to lock up political

Photo: Peter Trimming

prisoners and was where the King ordered the deaths of 24 French prisoners of war by starvation. However, his cruel streak aside, he did like the castle and spent somewhere in the region of £1,400 on doing it up and adding new apartments. When you take into account that a medium-size strong castle at that time would cost around £2,000 to build from scratch, you can see that John spent a vast sum of money. Incidentally, records tell that John liked life's finer things and was fastidious about personal cleanliness, so much so that he had a bath eight times between January and June in 1209!

In 1244, Henry III ordered the Corfe keep to be whitewashed, following in the footsteps of the Tower of London, which was whitewashed four years before.

Further down the line, Queen Elizabeth I sold the castle to her Lord Chancellor, Sir Christopher Hatton, in 1572. He in turn sold it in 1635 to Sir John Bankes, Attorney General to Charles I who bought it as a private residence. It suited the wealthy family who owned parts of the county of Dorset. In 1640, Sir John's status was given another boost when King Charles I appointed him Chief Justice of the Common Pleas. Sir John and his wife Lady Mary set about refurbishing the castle at great expense with spectacular tapestries, carpets, furniture, books and paintings.

On the outbreak of the Civil War in 1642, Sir John went off to support King Charles and the cavaliers against Oliver Cromwell's roundheads while Lady Mary and their younger daughters stayed at Corfe. In 1643, with a Royalist garrison of about 80 men, Lady Mary endured a siege of the castle by Parliamentary forces and became known as 'Brave Dame Mary'. Apparently, her courageousness included throwing stones and hot embers over the castle walls, so helping repel the rebels and prevent them from gaining access. That, together with the strength of the castle and the subsequent approach of Royalist forces, meant that the attackers failed in their attempts. However, some historians doubt whether Lady Mary was actually ever there at that time ...

Anyway, the castle wasn't so lucky during the second siege in 1645. It was plundered, the fine and fancy furnishings were removed and it was blown up.

After the Restoration of 1660 the Bankes family regained their property and it remained in their ownership for the next 3,500 years although they decided not to rebuild it. The ruined castle and surrounding land remained with the family until 1982 when Ralph Bankes gave the estate to the National Trust.

Interesting facts about Corfe Castle:

• Ravens nest at Corfe Castle and buzzards, falcons and redstarts can also be seen there.

• The original arrow slits and murder holes can still be seen in the castle walls. The murder holes were used for pouring boiling water or oil on anyone attacking the castle.

• Children's author Enid Blyton allegedly found inspiration from Corfe Castle and used it as the basis for Kirrin Island in her popular *Famous Five* book series.

Address: Corfe Castle, Wareham, Dorset, BH20 5EZ

Website: www.nationaltrust.org.uk/corfe-castle

Visitor information: Corfe Castle is managed by the National Trust. The castle regularly hosts events of various kinds including living history days when volunteers dress, eat and live as they would have done in Norman and medieval times.

Facilities include a gift shop, tea room, parking and information points.

HAMPTON COURT PALACE, SURREY

Built on the site of an 11th-century manor house, Hampton Court Palace was rebuilt in 1529 by King Henry VIII in a style to rival Versailles.

'Hampton Court is as noble and uniform a pile, and as capacious as any Gothic architecture can have made it … The great hall is a most magnificent room …' so said John Evelyn, diarist (1662).

The transformation of the 500-year-old Tudor palace was Cardinal Wolsey's doing. He intended to create a grand building where he could host not only the king and the royal court but also monarchs from across Europe. He spent enormous amounts of money but did ultimately create a palace fit for a king. In fact, he was so successful in his work that King Henry VIII eventually took Hampton Court for himself and, once he'd renovated and expanded, he went on to bring all his six wives here. It was one of his favourite residences and by the 1530s, besides being a magnificent palace, was also a hotel, theatre and vast leisure complex. The King's power shone through his lavish banquets and extravagant court life. There was accommodation for courtiers inside the palace while in the west front of the courtyard there were 30 suites of lodgings available for fine and fancy folks.

When William III and Mary II acceded to the throne in 1689, they commissioned Sir Christopher Wren to build a new baroque palace. The building included a special kitchen, the Chocolate Kitchen, because at the time chocolate was relatively new in England and an expensive luxury. The Chocolate Kitchen was a small but specialised series of rooms where royally-appointed chocolate makers prepared the expensive delicacy for the royals. They turned cocoa beans into chocolate cakes, a laborious process. 'Cakes' in this case mean 'pieces', which were stored on wax paper. Today visitors can see the equipment and examples of ingredients and different flavourings used. The inclusion of this kitchen in the new part of the palace demonstrated the wealth, power and modernity of William and Mary's court.

Later, Georgian kings and princes were forever in and out of Hampton Court and when the royals left in 1737 impoverished 'grace and favour' aristocrats moved in.

The palace is said to be haunted by Henry VIII's fifth wife Catherine Howard, who has been seen wandering restlessly through the rooms, as she probably did when she was there under house arrest after being charged with adultery. A story goes that she ran along the gallery to the chapel where the King was at Mass to beg his forgiveness, but before she could reach him, she was seized by guards and dragged screaming back to her rooms. Well, it was never a good bet to marry King Henry VIII, although he had showered her with jewels and genuinely cared for her until he thought she had been unfaithful to him with Thomas Culpepper. Culpepper also lost his head for his part in the alleged affair. Visitors are said to have heard her ghostly shrieks. Another phantom comes in the shape of Henry's third wife, Jane Seymour, who has been spotted

Photo: Joyofmuseums

walking in the cobbled grounds of Clock Court. On the anniversary of the birth of her son Edward, she is said to ascend the stairs leading to the Silver Stick Gallery, dressed in a white robe and carrying a candle.

Besides the phantoms, the palace is famous for its maze, planted in the 17th century. It covers a third of an acre, is trapezoid in shape and is the UK's oldest surviving hedge maze. In Jerome K. Jerome's *Three Men in a Boat* (1889) the maze gets a mention: 'We'll just go in here, so that you can say you've been, but it's very simple. It's absurd to call it a maze. You keep on taking the first turning to the right. We'll just walk around for ten minutes, and then go and get some lunch.' However, the character, Harris, leads the tourists into the maze and they subsequently get lost for hours.

Queen Victoria opened the palace to the public in 1838 and now it is one of six in the UK maintained by the Historic Royal Palaces charity.

Interesting facts about Hampton Court Palace:

• In William and Mary's time, the royals would usually take their chocolate as a breakfast drink. It was often served in the bedroom, as part of a ritual known as the levee, where the King or Queen would ceremoniously get dressed in front of a special chosen few.

• Henry VIII's kitchens at Hampton Court Palace were the largest in Tudor England. Two hundred cooks, sergeants, grooms and pages worked to produce over 800 meals a day for the King's household. It couldn't have been a very pleasant place to work though by all accounts because a Spanish visitor to the Tudor court in 1554 said the kitchens were 'veritable hells, such is the stir and bustle in them ...

there is plenty of beer here, and they drink more than would fill the Valladolid river'.

• William Shakespeare's company, the 'King's Men', performed in the palace for James I over Christmas and New Year 1603–4.

Address: Hampton Court Palace, East Molesey, Surrey KT8 9AU

Website: www.hrp.org.uk/hampton-court-palace

Visitor information: The palace is exceedingly visitor-friendly. Daily programmes are available and there are cafés and shopping facilities in the grounds. Regular themed events take place inside and outside. Buggies and pushchairs can be taken round the palace and there are dedicated facilities for the disabled with carer tickets and wheelchair hire available. It is advisable to wear sensible footwear when visiting due to uneven surfaces and cobbles.

The Magic Garden is where to get up close and personal with mythical beasts, besiege the towers and explore the secret grotto. The 250-year-old Great Vine, the world's largest grapevine, can also be marvelled at.

Besides Henry's private apartments and the vast Tudor kitchens, visitors can see England's oldest real tennis courts, where Henry played when he was a boy.

And where better to throw a party fit for a young king or queen? See website for arranging a child's birthday party with a difference.

LEEDS CASTLE, KENT

Confusingly, Leeds Castle is not in Leeds, but outside Maidstone in the English county of Kent. It is so named because around 850 the land was owned by a Saxon nobleman named Led or Leed who originally created a wooden structure on two islands in the River Len. Today the castle stands on the site of the Royal Manor, built in 857.

Listed in the Domesday Book, Leeds Castle has had many incarnations – as a Norman stronghold; a Jacobean country house; a Georgian mansion; and an elegant early 20th-century retreat for the rich and famous. It was also the private property of six medieval queens; Eleanor, Isabella, Philippa of Hainault (wife of Edward III), Joan of Navarre, Catherine de Valois and Catherine of Aragon. Elizabeth I was also imprisoned here for a time before her coronation. No wonder the castle is referred to as the 'Castle of Queens, Queen of Castles'.

The first stone castle on the site was built in 1119 by a Norman baron during the reign of William the Conqueror's son Henry I. The smaller of the two islands in the River Len was used to build the keep, while the larger island was used for the bailey. In 1278 it came into the possession of Queen Eleanor of Castile, Edward I's first wife, who acquired it in exchange for clearing the debts of one-time owner William de Leyburn. After Eleanor died, Edward gave it to his second wife, Queen Margaret of France. After she died in 1318 ownership again reverted to the Crown.

For the next three centuries the castle trundled along as a royal residence, before becoming a private home. A family called St Leger bought it in the 1550s and sold it in 1618 to a Sir Richard Smythe. It was subsequently handed down through a network of interlinked families.

In 1926 the castle was purchased by Anglo-American heiress Lady Baillie, who set about modernising it to suit her particular style. This society hostess liked to throw weekend house parties at the castle inviting politicians, aristocracy and stars of the silver screen including Errol Flynn, Charlie Chaplin, Douglas Fairbanks Jr. and David Niven. Lady Baillie also had a private cinema installed for her guests in the Maiden's Tower where there were also bachelor apartments.

In 1940 the castle was a temporary home for some ill-fated expeditionary forces who were repatriated after the retreat from Dunkirk. Severely burned pilots recuperated here too after being treated by Sir Archibald McIndoe at East Grinstead Hospital.

When Lady Baillie died in 1974 ownership of the castle was transferred to the Leeds Castle Foundation and it was subsequently opened to the public. Since then it has been used for a number of international events including the Northern Ireland peace talks in 2004.

Of course, Leeds Castle is something of a beauty queen and as you might expect has been the backdrop for film and television productions including the 1949 film *Kind Hearts and Coronets*; a BBC production of Shakespeare's *Henry VIII* in 1979; *Lady Jane* in 1986 starring Helena Bonham Carter; and in 2016 *The Hollow Crown: The Wars of the Roses* with Benedict Cumberbatch. TV shows filmed here include the BBC's *Bargain Hunt* and *Antiques Roadshow.*

One of the garden's most intriguing elements is the man-made maze. For starters, this wonder has over 2,000 yew trees and is square in shape. But here's the thing, when seen from above it looks circular! Fun indeed but it does add to the

problem of finding your way round. If you reach the centre, you'll see an amazing grotto representing the underworld which features mythical beasts painstakingly created from shells. The domed ceiling is decorated with black and white swans, symbols of alchemy and of Leeds Castle itself. The further in you go the designs become more macabre, with bones emerging from walls, fish flying and creatures encrusted on the walls walking upside down, and the whole thing is sprinkled with exotic minerals. Behind bars, guarding the final chamber, is the squatting figure of a life-sized mythical green man holding a bronze key. In legend the Green Man has pagan roots and symbolises woodland spirits and rebirth. He is there to ward off evil spirits.

The castle's one-time stables are a must-visit for dog lovers as this is where to find the Dog Collar Museum. It is crammed with a collection of historic collars spanning 500 years. The earliest, dating back to the late 15th century is a Spanish iron herd mastiff's collar, which would have been worn for protection against roaming wolves and bears. Others in the collection include ornate baroque gilt collars, 19th-century silver collars and 20th-century collars fashioned from tyres, beads and plastic. Your four-legged friend would love to have a sniff round here, but unfortunately, dogs are not admitted.

Interesting facts about Leeds Castle:

• King Henry VIII owned the castle for a time, transforming it into a home for his first wife, Catherine of Aragon. An inventory from 1532 notes that fireplaces were decorated with Spanish symbols. This reflected Catherine's nationality.

• In parkland surrounding the castle, streams and lakes

are home to over 30 species of waterfowl as well as being a habitat for ducks, geese and black swans.

• Lady Baillie was a trendsetter of her day and had a swimming pool in the grounds with England's first wave machine.

Address: Leeds Castle, Maidstone, Kent, ME17 1PL

Website: www.leeds-castle.com

Visitor information: Castle events are many and varied and include falconry displays, organ recitals, open-air concerts, vintage car rallies, medieval jousts, a triathlon and open-air cinema evenings. Adrenalin-fuelled activities include a ropes course for adults and juniors and there is a zip line. In winter, events include a fireworks party and Christmas and New Year celebrations.

Visitors should allow plenty of time to enjoy the castle and its 500 acres of gardens and parkland. However, if you don't get to see all you want on your first visit, admission tickets are valid for a year so you can return again to enjoy what was called 'the loveliest castle in the world' by picture-postcard historian Lord Conway in 1913.

The castle can be hired for weddings, conferences, banquets and all sorts of celebrations. It also has a nine-hole golf course. A number of outbuildings can be rented as holiday accommodation. The restaurant offers lunches and visitors can dine in the evening without purchasing an entry ticket.

PALACE OF WESTMINSTER (HOUSES OF PARLIAMENT), LONDON

In the early 8th century a Saxon church dedicated to St Peter was built on the site of the present Palace of Westminster. The church became known as the West Minster (west monastery), while St Paul's, lying to the east in the heart of London, was the East Minster (east monastery).

In the 10th century the church was reconstituted as a Benedictine abbey and adopted as a royal church. Royal interest in this abbey, both as a burial place and an expression of Christian kingship, prompted the construction of a palace at Westminster. Over the centuries, buildings have come and gone, but the palace has been in continuous existence in some form since the Danish King Cnut (1016–35) began building here in the first half of the 11th century.

After his coronation in 1042, St Edward the Confessor began building Westminster Abbey, which stands adjacent to the current Houses of Parliament. He built a palace nearby in order to oversee the construction of his new abbey. Edward lived in his new palace, but not for long and when he died was buried in his abbey in 1066.

There are few surviving sections of Edward's ancient Palace of Westminster, due to a fire in 1834, but most of these can be visited. The five surviving parts are Westminster Hall, the Jewel Tower, the Chapel of St Mary's Undercroft and the Cloisters and Chapter House of St Stephen's Chapel.

Nowadays, the Houses of Parliament, otherwise known as the Palace of Westminster, symbolise Great Britain and decisions made in its corridors of power have shaped the country past and present. This fat history book of a building is the meeting place of the House of Commons and the House of Lords. Much of how Parliament does its business has become established through continued use over the centuries. This is known as 'custom and practice'. There are ancient rules and traditions which still have to be adhered to, some of which seem to have no relevance to life today. Let's have a look at some of the most peculiar:

Smoking has not been allowed in the chamber of the House of Commons since the 17th century. Members could however take snuff and the doorkeepers still keep a snuff box for this purpose.

Members may not eat or drink in the chamber, though there is an exception to this rule. The Chancellor of the Exchequer is allowed to have an alcoholic drink while delivering the Budget statement.

While the House of Commons is in session it is illegal for a Member of Parliament (MP) to wear a full suit of armour (yes, I agree, unlikely these days). They are not allowed to wear military decorations either.

Before every sitting of the House, the Speaker's procession leaves the Speaker's House inside the Palace of Westminster and heads for the Commons chamber. A doorkeeper and the Serjeant at Arms carrying the mace walk ahead of the Speaker. Some members of the Speaker's staff, including his chaplain, secretary and a trainbearer, follow behind. As the procession reaches the central lobby, a policeman shouts: 'Hats off strangers!' This is the call for helmeted policemen and any members of the public wearing hats to remove their headgear as the procession passes.

Parliament's status as a royal palace allows MPs to play roulette in the lobbies.

When a new Speaker of the House of Commons is elected,

Photo: Bjørn Erik Pedersen

other Members physically drag the successful candidate to the chair. This custom has its roots in the Speaker's function to communicate the Commons' opinions to the monarch. Historically, if the monarch disagreed with the message being communicated, the early death of the Speaker could follow. It is perhaps little wonder that Speakers of old were reluctant to accept the post.

And a footnote about beautiful Westminster Hall: merchandise was sold here by the late 1200s. The Keeper of the Palace was entitled to rent of eight pence a year from each merchant who had a booth in the hall and he received four pence a year from every merchant carrying his goods. By the reign of Richard II (1377–99), the hall had become one of the chief centres of London life. Due to the presence of the law courts, it also became a covered market for legal paraphernalia. Various shops and stalls sold wigs, pens and stationery. In the mid-1600s there were 48 shops in the Hall. Allowing space for the law courts, each shop must have been about eight feet wide. These stalls were removed for coronation banquets and restored afterwards.

From 1189 to 1821 Westminster Hall was the traditional venue for coronation banquets honouring newly-crowned monarchs. The earliest recorded are those of Prince Henry, who was crowned in the lifetime of his father, Henry II, in 1170 and Richard the Lionheart in 1189.

The coronation feast of James II on 23 April 1685 was a huge event with an extensive menu and space for spectators in the galleries above the tables. Prior to the day, courts and shops were removed and the hall furnished with the royal table at the top of the stairs and two rows of tables stretching almost to the north door. Along the sides of the hall sixteen cupboards held dishes and cutlery.

On the day, participants had to arrive by 8am and were

marshalled into the hall. When the King and Queen entered the hall at 11.30am, they were presented with the sword of state and the coronation regalia and were subsequently borne in procession to Westminster Abbey. Once the procession had departed, tables were laid and cold food set out. Once the coronation service in the abbey was over, the King and Queen returned to the hall for the banquet where they sat at the royal table, wearing their crowns. Other tables held peers and peeresses, bishops, judges, barons, the King's Council, the Lord Mayor and heralds; there would have been about 200 servants – each nobleman also had one of his own servants present. The first course, consisting of 46 dishes of hot meat, was brought in by 73 people, including three officers on horseback. They don't do things like that anymore.

And a fun footnote: in Victorian times there was a ballad about the Houses of Parliament which told of a Hackney coachman who fell down the House of Commons privy: 'They said, Bill are you dead, no I'm only inturd.' Oh dear.

Interesting facts about the Palace of Westminster:

• Suffragette Emily Davidson hid for 48 hours in the Crypt under Westminster Hall, so that she could use 'House of Commons' as her address in that year's census.

• Members must not keep their hands in their pockets when in the Chamber. Andrew Robathan was heckled by opposing MPs when he did this on 19 December 1994.

• The only animals allowed in the Palace of Westminster are guide dogs for the blind, sniffer dogs, police horses and horses from the royal stables.

Address: Palace of Westminster, London SW1A OAA

Website:
www.parliament.uk/about/living-heritage/building/palace

Visitor information: Open to visitors year-round to attend debates and committee hearings in the House of Commons and House of Lords.

Visitors can book guided tours or audio tours and these can be combined with afternoon tea. Both adult and children's menus are available, the latter including kiddie treats such as fruit jelly, milkshakes and Big Ben-shaped shortbread biscuits.

UK residents can arrange a tour through their MP or a member of the House of Lords. When the Houses are sitting the full tour may not be available.

THE TOWER OF LONDON, LONDON

This royal palace and secure fortress has served as a prison, armoury, treasury, menagerie and home of the Royal Mint. Besides that, it was the royal observatory, public records office and, since 1303, home of the Crown Jewels.

The Tower of London, a UNESCO World Heritage Site, is made up of numerous buildings within the inner walls. These are dominated by the White Tower, the original square fortress built by William the Conqueror in 1077. In due course, Henry III and Edward I expanded the fortress, adding defensive walls with a series of smaller towers. The moat was enlarged too. In its heyday, the Tower was home to all of England's monarchs down to James I. Medieval royals lived luxuriously in the Tower. They worshipped in the Chapel Royal, kept a menagerie of exotic animals and welcomed foreign rulers at ceremonial occasions.

The Tower was believed to be unassailable, that was until the Peasants' Revolt in 1381, a result of the introduction of a new 'poll' tax by Richard II's government. Led by Wat Tyler, 20,000 rebels marched on the capital and headed straight for the Tower of London. The King agreed to meet them but perhaps should have been a little more cautious because as soon as the gates were opened to let him out, 400 rebels rushed in. They ran hell for leather and reached the innermost areas of the fortress, headed for the second floor of the White Tower, and burst into St John's Chapel, where they found the Archbishop of Canterbury. They took him and his companions to Tower Hill where they killed them straightaway. Records say it took eight blows from the axe to cut off the archbishop's head and then they stuck it on top of a pole on London Bridge as a warning to others not to upset them.

Because beheadings, murders, torture, hangings and all manner of grisly things happened in here, it's hardly surprising that a phantom or two lingers within its stone walls. In the past 900 years the building has developed the reputation of being one of Britain's most haunted places. Points for most persistent ghost go to Queen Anne Boleyn, beheaded on Tower Green in 1536. She has been seen near the Queen's House, close to the site of her execution and sometimes she leads a ghostly procession down the aisle of the Chapel Royal of St Peter ad Vincula. She is buried under the chapel's altar. Spookier still, her headless body has been seen walking the corridors of the Tower.

Photo: Tony Hisgett

The Bloody Tower was the scene of the infamous disappearance of the two young princes; twelve-year-old Edward V and ten-year-old Richard, Duke of York, sons of King Edward IV. No one knows exactly what happened to them, but they were more than likely murdered on the instructions of their uncle, the Duke of Gloucester. He was determined to wear the crown and didn't want anyone spoiling it for him. Centuries later, two children's skeletons were uncovered and as they were thought to be the remains of the princes were given a royal burial. Today they are among the most poignant ghosts in the Tower of London, and there are reports that they have been seen on the stairs.

There's explorer and adventurer Sir Walter Raleigh too, who was assigned two rooms on the second floor of the Bloody Tower and lived there for thirteen years. The rooms are still furnished as they were when he was there. He was freed to look for the lost city of El Dorado but when he didn't come up with the goods was taken back to prison again. Although he was executed in Old Palace Yard at Westminster, visitors have reported seeing his ghost looking as he does in his portrait hanging in the Bloody Tower.

And an interesting endnote to this section on the Tower's ghosts, Major General Geoffrey Field was governor of the Tower from 1994–2006. He and his family lived in The Queen's House on Tower Green. He said: 'Soon after we arrived in 1994, my wife was making up the bed in the Lennox Room when she was violently pushed right out of the room. No one had warned us that the house was haunted but we then discovered that every resident has experienced something strange in that room. The story goes that the ghost is that of Arabella Stuart, a cousin of James I, who was imprisoned and possibly murdered in that bedroom. Several women who slept there reported waking in terror in the middle of the night feeling they were being strangled, so just in case, we made it a house rule not to give unaccompanied female guests the Lennox Room.' Sensible decision.

The Tower is steeped in legend, but one of the most famous involves the ravens. The story goes that six ravens must remain for all time at the Tower, and should they ever leave, both the Tower and the kingdom will fall. Seven ravens – that's six and a spare – live at the Tower today and are cared for by a dedicated Yeoman Warder known as the Ravenmaster. The birds have one flight feather trimmed to stop them flying away.

When night falls, the gates are locked and all the visitors have gone, the Tower embraces a thriving community within its walls. It is home to the Yeomen Warders and their families, the resident governor as well as a garrison of soldiers. There is a doctor, a chaplain and a pub too!

In 2014, to mark the centenary of the beginning of the First World War, the tower moat was filled with 888,246 ceramic poppies, each one representing a British or colonial military fatality during the conflict. 'Blood Swept Lands and Seas of Red' became one of London's most iconic landmarks and was visited by millions of people from around the world.

Interesting facts about the Tower of London:

• In 1240, Henry III had the Tower's great keep painted white, hence its name – the White Tower.

• Henry VII's personal guards were the first 'Beefeaters', who could eat as much beef as they wanted from the king's table. Today the Beefeaters, properly called Yeomen Warders, still carry out ceremonial duties, including unlocking and locking the Tower every day in the Ceremony of the Keys.

• One prisoner in the Tower was Hitler's right-hand man, Rudolf Hess, who was brought to London in May 1941 after landing in Scotland. He may have landed on a peace mission though no one knows for sure.

Address: The Tower of London, London EC3N 4AB

Website: www.hrp.org.uk/tower-of-london

Visitor information: The Tower is open daily with free entry for carers. For wheelchair users, a colour map is available detailing routes. Within the complex there are shops and four dining options to choose from. The Tower and its legendary guardians, the pampered ravens, attract in the region of 3 million visitors a year.

WARWICK CASTLE, WARWICKSHIRE

Medieval history, magic and myth, it's all here at William the Conqueror's castle. As well as being a crown property under seven monarchs, the castle has had more than 30 owners. They were an unfortunate bunch really because at least three of them died in battle, two were executed and one was murdered.

Not that William's motte and bailey castle, built to keep control of the midlands as he advanced northwards, was the first fortification on this spot. That honour goes to a rampart of earth constructed on the orders of Alfred the Great's daughter Ethelfleda in 914, as one of ten in the Kingdom of Mercia aimed at fending off the Vikings.

In 1153, the wife of Roger de Beaumont, 2nd Earl of Warwick, made a huge mistake when she gave the castle to the invading army of Henry of Anjou (later Henry II). They told her that her husband had been killed. Awful. A terrible situation, which got worse when the not-yet-dead Roger de Beaumont heard what she had done – then he died of shock on the spot. However perhaps Henry suffered a degree of remorse for his dastardly deed, because later he returned the castle to the Earls of Warwick.

In 1260 the wooden Norman fortress was rebuilt in stone. Four years later Warwick was besieged by supporters of rebel Simon de Montfort who captured the current Earl, William Maudit and took him and his wife to be imprisoned at Kenilworth Castle.

In 1312, Piers Gaveston, the exiled 1st Earl of Cornwall, was imprisoned in Warwick Castle. He was a favourite pal of Edward II and his exclusive access to the royal household caused anger and resentment among the nobility. He was captured, imprisoned in the castle and subsequently executed at Blacklow Hill near Warwick. A stone cross marks the spot. Meanwhile, Edward II is famously rumoured to have been executed by the insertion of a red-hot poker.

The castle has a Ghost Tower, originally built in the 14th century, to prevent attack from the river. As the name suggests, it is said to be haunted – by the ghost of Sir Fulke Greville who died in 1628. He lived in the tower whenever he came to visit Warwick and he was murdered in London by his servant, Ralph Haywood, who found out that his master was going to leave him a pittance in his will. However, he obviously did it hastily, because as soon as he realised what he had done, he killed himself.

Visitors can explore the state rooms and see a waxwork exhibit called the Royal Weekend Party. This depicts a

Photo: DeFacto

typical event which would have been held at the castle in days gone by. There are also waxworks of all the earls who lived here, including Richard Neville, 16th Earl of Warwick, called the 'Kingmaker', who helped imprison Edward IV in the castle. He got this name due to his meddling in matters of the succession. Richard originally fought to make his cousin Edward IV king, but later switched sides and tried to restore the Lancastrian heir, Edward VI, son of Henry VI, as king. Richard's quarrels with Edward IV began over the King's marriage to Elizabeth Woodville.

The Capability Brown-designed gardens are pretty, particularly the Victorian Rose Garden which has a canopy and a waterfall. Just off the garden path are icehouses; subterranean chambers where blocks of ice preserved food in the days before refrigerators or freezers were invented. There is the formal Peacock Garden too, it has four large topiary peacock-shaped hedges as well as real peacocks and peahens strutting around.

At the base of the castle walls is the old Engine House, site of a water mill that ground grain for the castle in the 15th century. In the late 19th century the mill was converted into an engine house, using the river to generate electrical power for the castle. Electrical equipment was installed in 1894 and the castle wired for power, making it one of the earliest places in the country to be lit by electric lights. Four-hundred-and-seventy-five of them, in case you're wondering.

Interesting facts about Warwick Castle:

• This is where to view the most powerful catapult in the world. Called a 'trebuchet', this medieval launching weapon is roughly the height of three houses. In 2006 it launched a thirteen-kilogram missile 240 metres – the length of ten tennis courts, at a speed of 257 kilometres per hour. Visitors can see it in action as it shoots twice daily from April to October. It fires a 22-kilogram stone projectile, which lands approximately 200 metres from its release point, in a designated landing area within the wider castle grounds. This area is marshalled and not accessible to the public either during firing or at other times.

• The castle has hosted many royals over the centuries, some as guests, others as prisoners. Queen Elizabeth I visited in 1566 and liked it enough to return in 1572 when she stayed for four nights. In 1868, Queen Victoria visited the castle; Diana, Princess of Wales came on 8 July 1986 and HM Queen Elizabeth II visited in 1997.

• In medieval times falconry was an important sport at the castle. In those days it was as popular as tennis or golf is today. The birds that people owned were a status symbol and punishments for stealing a bird above your station were severe, including amputation. Servants, knaves and children could only own kestrels and hawks. Eagles were for the nobility.

Address: Warwick Castle, Warwick CV34 4QU

Website: www.warwick-castle.com

Visitor information: The castle is now a theme park owned by Merlin Entertainments who also own Madame Tussauds waxworks museum in London and the London Eye. This means there are lots of interactive attractions and walk-through adventures, daily shows, falconry displays and jousting tournaments featuring the Devil's Horsemen (a company who provide horses, riders and carriages to the film industry), whose film credits include *Braveheart* (1995),

Tomb Raider (2003) and *Troy* (2004). Besides that there are guided tours especially arranged for children.

The mighty castle itself is, thankfully, still the centrepiece. What would William the Conqueror think if he came back and saw it now?

WINDSOR CASTLE, BERKSHIRE

Windsor Castle is the world's oldest and largest occupied castle. The castle grounds cover 52,609 square metres (thirteen acres).

It was William the Conqueror who chose the site, high above the River Thames on the edge of a Saxon hunting ground, around 1070. It took a day to march from the Tower of London to Windsor and the castle guarded the western approach to the capital.

The wooden castle was rebuilt by Edward III in the mid-1300s as a Gothic palace and cost him the huge sum – in those days – of £50,000. *Holinshed Chronicles* recorded: 'this year, 1359, the Kyng sette workemenne in hande to take downe much olde buildings belonging to the Castel of Windsor, and caused divers other faires and sumptuous works to bee erected and sette up in and about the same Castel, so that almost all the masons and carpenters that were of any accounte within this lande were sente for …'

The King delighted in tournaments which allowed him and his court to wear elaborate costumes and crests. One that he wore in 1339 contained 3,000 peacock feathers. The banners of today's Knights of the Garter in the Quire of St George's Chapel descend from those origins.

Further down the line, during the English Civil War, Oliver Cromwell used the castle as his headquarters. When Charles II was crowned king in 1660, the year of the restoration of the monarchy, he appointed architect Hugh May to supervise modernising the apartments. It took eleven years for the work to be completed but they became the grandest baroque state apartments in England. The new apartments created for the King and his Queen, Catherine of Braganza, followed the pattern that had evolved over the years. Each set of rooms started with a heavily armed guard chamber – this was a visual reminder for visitors that the royals were well guarded. Then one after another was the Presence Chamber, Privy Chamber, Withdrawing Room, Great Bedchamber, Little Bedchamber and Closet. The King ordered that 'all persons … of quality and good fortune' and 'all wives and daughters of nobility' should be allowed to pass into the Presence Chamber. He loved Windsor dearly but didn't like to be outshone by his cousin, Louis XIV of France, who had used architectural magnificence at Versailles and the Louvre to demonstrate his importance. He therefore copied his cousin by creating a playhouse at Windsor which came with a troupe of French players and music from a new court orchestra called the 'Twenty-Four Violins'.

When George IV succeeded to the throne in 1820, he set about organising the addition of more battlements and heightening Henry II's Round Tower by 30 feet to improve the castle's skyline and to underline his wish for more Gothic exuberance. The cost was almost £300,000. Thanks to the improvements, his successor Queen Victoria didn't need to do much at all to the castle and it became principal palace of the British monarchy and focus of the British Empire during her reign.

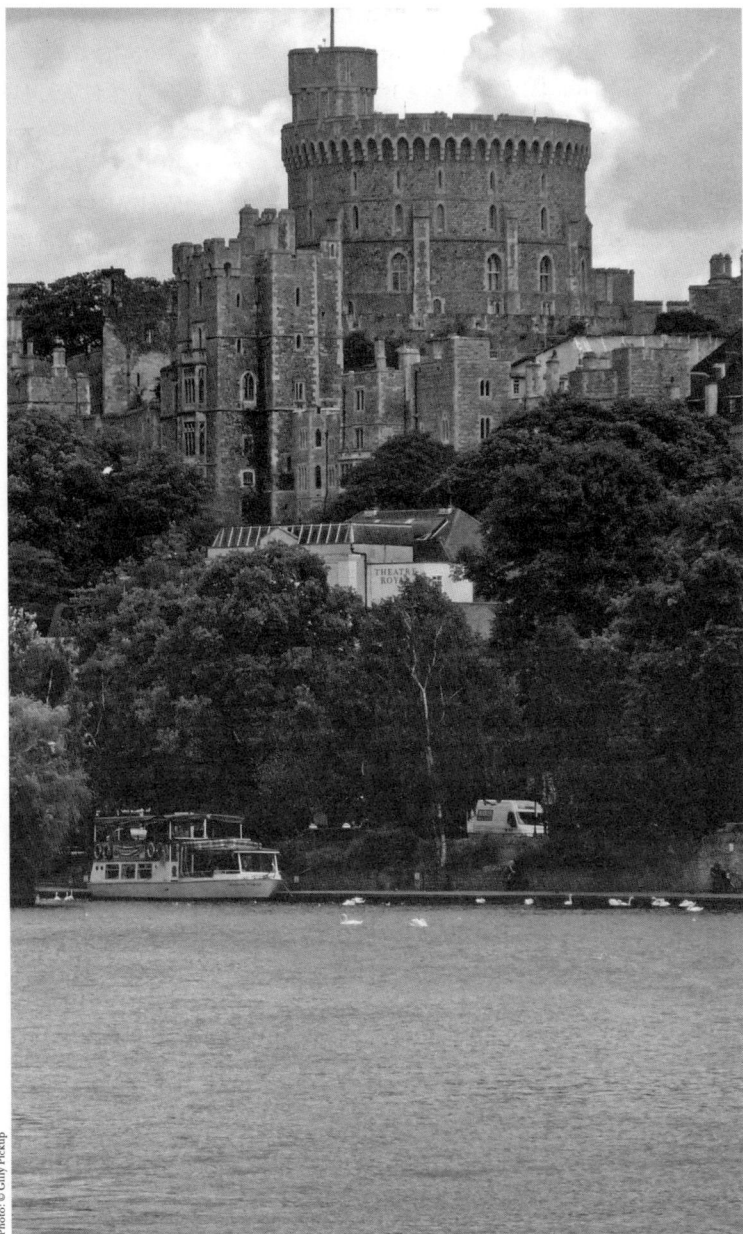

Photo: © Gilly Pickup

When George VI came to the throne he and Queen Elizabeth considered Windsor very much their home. They remained at Buckingham Palace during the aerial bombardment – they didn't desert the people of London – but joined their daughters Elizabeth (now Queen Elizabeth II) and Margaret at Windsor in the evenings and weekends. Every Christmas the girls performed a pantomime in the castle's Waterloo Chamber.

Windsor Castle is still so special for HM Queen Elizabeth II that she spends most of her private weekends there. She takes up official residence at Easter and for a week in June when she attends Royal Ascot and the service of the Order of the Garter in St George's Chapel in the Castle Precincts. St George's Chapel is the resting place of ten monarchs including Henry VIII, Charles I and George V.

The State Apartments are magnificent and include St George's Hall, the biggest room in the castle and where state banquets are held. There's also Waterloo Chamber, built to honour the victory over Napoleon and of course many smaller, more intimate rooms. Furnishings include important works of art by Rembrandt, Rubens, Holbein and Van Dyck, as well as French and English furniture and porcelain. The Grand Reception Room used to be the main ballroom, and one of the most wonderful pieces on display here is a malachite urn, presented to Queen Victoria by Tsar Nicholas I in 1839 – one of the largest examples outside Russia.

The castle did not suffer damage during the Second World War – there is a story that Hitler wanted to make it his home if he won the war so issued orders that it mustn't be bombed – but 50 years later, on 20 November 1992, a huge fire broke out in Queen Victoria's Private Chapel. It is thought to have been caused by a spotlight igniting a curtain. The fire spread rapidly through the roof spaces, destroying the ceiling of

St George's Hall and the Grand Reception Room as well as gutting the State Dining Room, Crimson Drawing Room, the Private Chapel and dozens of ancillary rooms. It took 200 firefighters fifteen hours and 1.5 million gallons of water to extinguish the flames. Repair work was completed on 20 November 1997, exactly five years after the outbreak of the fire and on the Golden Wedding Anniversary of HM Queen Elizabeth II and the Duke of Edinburgh. It cost £37 million to repair, supplemented by funds from the parliamentary grant for the castle's maintenance, but largely met from proceeds of admissions to the castle and to Buckingham Palace, which was opened to the public for the first time in 1993.

Interesting facts about Windsor Castle:

• Clocks in the Great Kitchen are kept five minutes fast to ensure that the food served to Her Majesty is never late. The kitchen whisk meanwhile, can hold up to 250 eggs at one time and 18,000 bottles of wine are kept in the cellar.

• Henry VIII's armour is on display in the Lantern Lobby. Several 'exchange' pieces, to adapt the armour to suit the different exercises of tournaments, are displayed in the Queen's Guard Chamber.

• Soldiers on sentry duty are usually drawn from the five regiments of Foot Guards including Coldstream, Grenadier and Scots, Welsh and Irish Guards. The Changing of the Guard takes place at 11am on Monday through Saturday from April until the end of July and on alternating days for the rest of the year.

Address: Windsor Castle, Berkshire, SL4 1NJ

Website: www.rct.uk/visit/windsorcastle

Visitor information: Day and evening tours of the State Apartments are available throughout the year. Dates vary depending on when the Royal Family is in residence. Visitors can also walk around Queen Mary's Dolls' House and see inside each room filled with thousands of objects on the tiny scale of one:twelve. The library is full of original works by top literary names of the day, there is a fully stocked wine cellar and a garden created by Gertrude Jekyll. The Dolls' House has electricity, running hot and cold water, working lifts and flushing lavatories.

When visitors first arrive they can join a free 30-minute tour of the Castle Precincts led by wardens. They depart regularly throughout the day from the Courtyard.

– IRELAND –

BLARNEY CASTLE, COUNTY CORK

This castle, a medieval stronghold, is probably most famous for its Blarney Stone, said to give the 'gift of the gab' to anyone who kisses it. The word 'blarney' has come to mean 'flattering' or 'smooth talk'.

The castle dates way back, from before AD 1200 in fact. It was destroyed in 1446 by fire, and rebuilt by Cormac MacCarthy, King of Munster. These days it is a partial ruin with some accessible rooms and battlements. However, its walls are still twelve feet thick in places, which would have afforded great protection from invaders during battle.

There are legends galore as to the origin of the Blarney Stone. Was it the Lia Fáil, a stone with mystical powers upon which Irish kings were crowned around AD 500? This stone's powers were revealed to the MacCarthys by a witch who had been saved from drowning. Or was it half of the original Stone of Scone, said to have been presented to Cormac MacCarthy by Robert the Bruce in 1314, in gratitude and recognition of his support in the Battle of Bannockburn? (For more on the Stone of Scone, see *Edinburgh Castle*.)

Ah, perhaps it was the stone Jacob used as a pillow. No? Well could it have been St. Columba's pillow, the one he used on his deathbed. Nonsense! It was the Stone of Ezel, which David hid behind while fleeing from King Saul and it could have been brought to Ireland during the Crusades. Or maybe it was the stone that Moses struck with his staff to produce water for the Israelites, during their flight from Egypt in Ireland? I guess we'll never know its history for sure, although in 2014 geologists confirmed that the stone was sourced from 330 million-year-old limestone and that it couldn't have come from England. Molecular samples said that the rock was native to southern Ireland.

For over 200 years world statesmen, authors, painters and legends of the silver screen have joined those climbing the 128 stone steps to kiss the Blarney Stone and gain the gift of eloquence.

In the past, visitors had to be held by the ankles and lowered over the battlements to kiss the Blarney Stone. It is easier and safer today; you lie on the parapet walk and lean backwards while holding onto a set of iron bars. There is an attendant on hand to hold your legs just to make sure that you won't fall. That way you can give the stone an upside down kiss. It's always wise to be careful though, more so if

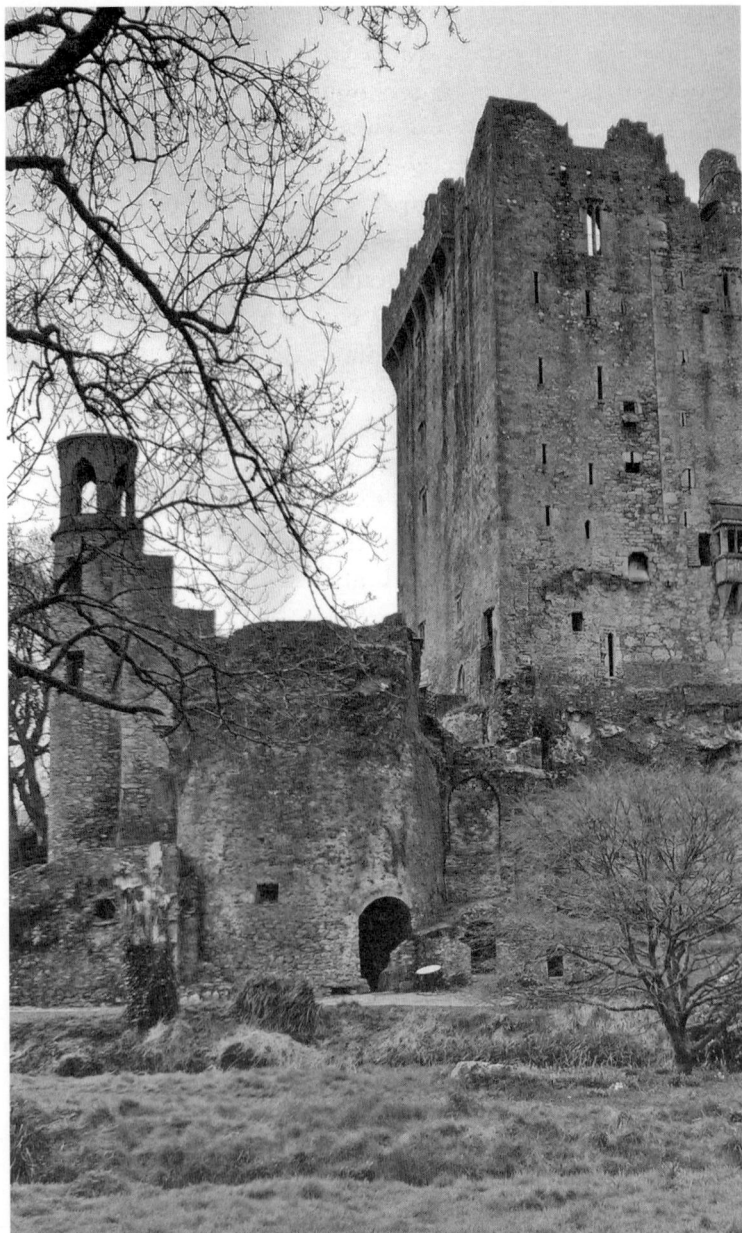

Photo: Kompal

there is someone nearby who doesn't like you very much. But perhaps that's the least of your worries after you have kissed a surface which many thousands of others have kissed before you. I'm thinking of those germs ... although when the crowds thin out, the guy I mentioned earlier, the one who holds onto your legs, sprays the stone with stuff from a bottle of anti-bacterial cleanser.

Anyway, there's more potential danger if you visit the Poison Garden. At its entrance a sign warns visitors: 'Do not touch, smell, or eat any plant'. Well wouldn't that just be asking for trouble? Opened in 2010, this collection of over 70 flora contains toxic shrubs including henbane, hemlock, wormwood and cannabis. As the old saying goes, 'It will either kill you or cure you' ... However, the deadliest specimens are locked away in cages so no harm will befall the visitor who just comes to look and admire.

Walking round the lovely gardens you'll come across rock formations, including the Wishing Steps and the Witch's Kitchen, which has a chimney and fireplace. This is believed to have been a prehistoric dwelling dating back around 3,000 years or even more. They say the witch is trapped within the stone ... . There is a dolmen – megalithic grave – here too. And of course since this is Ireland, you would almost expect to find wish-granting waterfalls! To make a wish here is almost as difficult as kissing the Blarney Stone though: you have to walk backwards with your eyes closed down a rather steep set of stairs carved into a rock. If you make it in one piece, the waterfall at the bottom will grant your wish.

Arboreta grow collections of rare trees including magnolia, Japanese bamboo and Siberian dogwood and as you'd expect in this magical environment there's a little kissing tree with branches that grow upside down. Isn't that just grand?

Interesting facts about Blarney Castle:

• The Blarney Stone was put in position at the castle – 85 feet above ground on the battlement east wall – in 1446.

• Blarney Village is one of the last estate villages still in Ireland. It was built by an 18th-century landlord so that the castle workers had somewhere to live.

• A 'murder room' located just above the castle's main entrance proved crucial in warding off potential intruders. When unwanted visitors happened along, the guard hurled rocks or boiling oil, or indeed both, through a square hole in the floor. That ensured they wouldn't be bothered with those particular intruders again.

Address: Blarney Castle, Blarney, Co. Cork

Website: https://blarneycastle.ie

Visitor information: Blarney Castle is open to the public year-round. Tickets include entry to the castle and gardens. Make sure you kiss the stone when you visit and you'll never be lost for words again!

MALAHIDE CASTLE, COUNTY DUBLIN

Malahide Castle near Dublin was in the ownership of one family for nearly 800 years. Besides its stunning rooms, fine paintings, antique furniture and strollable gardens, several phantoms call the castle home.

The original structure was built in 1185 when King Henry II gave Richard Talbot the lands and harbour of Malahide. It was a generous gift, a thank you present because the knight had helped the King out several times. The Talbot family moved into the castle and grew to become one of Ireland's most powerful families. It was their home throughout the centuries until 1975.

Following the death in 1973 of Milo, the last Lord Talbot, his unmarried sister Rose sold the castle to the Irish government for 650,000 Irish pounds, partly to pay off death duties. The sale did not include contents, which were then auctioned over three days. After acquiring the castle, the local authority managed to buy back much of the furniture and paintings and subsequently expanded the fine collection.

In the meantime 60-year-old Rose left Ireland for another Malahide, a sheep farm in Tasmania owned by the family, where she lived until her death in 2009. The castle's renowned ghosts, however, remained in the castle and grounds.

Nothing remains of the original structure as the Talbot family were more interested in creating a home which met their changing needs rather than preserving history. The oldest surviving part is probably the three-storey tower, containing the Great Hall. It goes back a long way, to around 1400, and was the hub of family life. Entertainment was obviously a big thing to the Talbots as the table seats over twenty diners. There is also a minstrel gallery.

The castle also has strong links to the 1690 Battle of the Boyne, fought between Protestant King William of Orange and Catholic James II. Richard Talbot was James' Lord Lieutenant of Ireland and on the morning of the battle, fourteen Talbots and their relatives gathered for breakfast in the Great Hall. None of them returned.

Later extensions to the castle included the Oak Room,

a four-storey west wing and a library with golden-hued leather wallpaper decorated with flowers, butterflies and dragonflies. This style of wall hanging, often referred to as Spanish leatherwork, flourished between 1650 and 1700. Few genuine examples remain today and it is not certain whether that in the library is original.

On the ground floor in the 16th-century west-wing, visitors can amble between large and small drawing rooms which were originally one large room divided into four by tapestries. Objects to admire here include 18th-century plaster ceilings and the Malahide Orange-painted walls, a remarkable though perhaps garish colour, but certainly one of the glories of the castle. The large drawing room, originally used for more formal occasions, later became a family room. Furniture in here includes an oddly-shaped couch, known as a confidante. Its *raison d'être* that, should an unmarried lady wish to sit with her suitor, a chaperone would sit between them. Killjoy!

It's hardly surprising that a building of this age should harbour a ghost or two and Malahide Castle certainly delivers on this topic. There are seven in total. One of the scariest is that of English politician and roundhead Miles Corbet, the last (important) man to sign King Charles I's death warrant. He supported Oliver Cromwell because he wanted Britain to be a republic.

During his rise, Oliver Cromwell drove the Catholic Talbot family out of their castle and gave the property to the Catholic-hating Corbet. Most locals living near Malahide Castle were Catholic so Corbet outlawed the religion in the area and burned down the abbey. As they say though, what goes around comes around and he was caught by King Charles' men a couple of years later and unceremoniously returned to Malahide Castle where he was hanged, drawn and quartered. Since then, Corbet's ghost roams round the

Photo: Jean Housen

castle appearing most often on the anniversary of his death. His shade has also appeared at other times when those who have seen him say that he falls apart into bloody quarters – that's how he was killed.

Some ghosts prefer to stay outside, as do the two old ladies sometimes seen in the grounds – who they are is yet to be confirmed. Back inside, a woman in a white dress whose picture once hung in the Great Hall leaves her portrait occasionally to explore the rooms and corridors.

There's Walter Hussey too, a cavalier who ended up in Malahide as a soldier fighting the roundheads. During his stay, he fell in love with a local girl, and asked to marry her. Hussey's father travelled to Malahide to ask the Talbots if his son could hold the wedding ceremony at the castle. Everything was agreed and Hussey gave up battling the roundheads to stay in Malahide with his bride-to-be. However, he was ambushed while travelling to the castle on his wedding day. A spear thrown by a rival roundhead killed him. And can you believe it, after that his wife-to-be fell in love with his murderer, and married him instead! There's no understanding some folk. Walter's ghost has been seen several times, showing his spear wound to shocked visitors.

Puck, who had dwarfism, was the Talbot family jester during the Tudor era. He was also watchman for the tower prison. Lady Elenora Fitzgerald was sent to the tower prison by Henry VIII and it was Puck's job to keep an eye on her. Within weeks, he had fallen madly in love with her. He didn't tell anyone but rumours started to spread. The Talbots got to hear that someone was 'on the side' of Fitzgerald – they had to keep that news from the king, what if he thought it was them? As a result, on a cold December morning, Puck's murdered body was found outside the castle. The Talbots had taken matters into their own hands.

Family members claimed that Puck had killed himself – well wasn't he heartbroken because of unrequited love? There weren't many locals who believed this though. Puck had said shortly before his death that his ghost would haunt the castle, but wouldn't hurt anyone as long as a male Talbot lived there. Puck haunts the area leading to the Great Hall. Various Talbot family members have seen him and in 1976, when contents were being auctioned, he was spotted by an employee of Sotheby's auction house. He often seems to appear in tourists' photos, as a small, blurred figure, with unrecognisable features.

The castle's Botanic Garden, one of Ireland's finest, has been restored, the grounds developed and expanded. The walled garden was created around 1775 for growing herbs, fruit and vegetables and has been in use ever since.

Inside and out, Malahide Castle intrigues and delights and, who knows, you may even see one of its famous ghosts.

Interesting facts about Malahide Castle:

• The name Talbot originated in Northern France and comes from the old German name for a messenger – *talabod*.

• Part of the garden includes 22 acres of woodland, with some ancient trees including a Cedar of Lebanon believed to be over 350 years old.

• The Avoca café and shop in the courtyard offers a merry hub of shopping opportunities – gifts, homeware, fashion. Avoca Handweavers is a family-owned craft design company producing woven fabrics and signature throws and knits which are the company's hallmark.

Address: Malahide Castle and Gardens, Malahide, Co. Dublin

Website: www.malahidecastleandgardens.ie

Visitor information: The coastal town of Malahide is ten miles north of Dublin and around the same distance from Dublin international airport. Bus routes 32 and 42 go from Dublin to Malahide in around 40 minutes or travel by DART train in approximately 30 minutes. The castle is open to visitors year-round, except 24–26 December.

– NORTHERN IRELAND –

HILLSBOROUGH CASTLE, COUNTY DOWN

This working royal palace is the official residence of the British royals when they are in Northern Ireland and has been the home of the Secretary of State for Northern Ireland since the 1970s.

The mansion, thirteen miles from Belfast, was built in the 1770s by Wills Hill, first Marquis of Downshire. It was later remodelled in the 19th and early 20th centuries and was a family home for the Hills, who were Ireland's most important landowners at one time. They made improvements to the house adding a library, billiards room and offices and improved the servants' quarters.

In 1837 Hillsborough was the scene of the marriage of Lord Hillsborough, eldest son of the third Marquess, Arthur Hill. Guests at the extravagant event included around 3,500 tenants from the family's estates as well as 500 other guests. This event on the parade ground was reported in the *Ulster Times* as 'a fête … almost without parallel in the kingdom'. The ale flowed freely to the extent that thirteen guests succumbed to alcohol poisoning. There was even a verse written to describe it: 'the tables were spread, with roast beef and mutton, plum pudding and bread, and 3,500 to dinner sat down, a magnificent party for Hillsborough town.'

However, during the 1800s the family started to use Hillsborough less frequently and eventually they rented it out privately. Following the Irish Free State Act in 1922, the position of Lord Lieutenant became that of 'governor', with Hillsborough Castle being renamed Government House. Further along the line, in December 1924, the British government bought Hillsborough for £25,000, around £1.3 million in today's money, from the 6th Marquis, to be the residence of the governor of Northern Ireland.

There was a fire at Hillsborough in 1934 which meant a lot of rebuilding had to be done. Earl Granville, HM Queen Elizabeth's uncle, took the position as governor in 1945 and Her Majesty, the Queen Mother and Princess Margaret would come for holidays.

Over the years, Hillsborough has welcomed many important visitors. The link with the British royal family began in 1933 when Princess Alice, a granddaughter of Queen Victoria paid a visit. In March 1946, Princess Elizabeth, now HM the Queen, made her first solo visit to Northern Ireland to launch Harland and Wolff's new ship HMS Eagle. She stayed at Hillsborough Castle with her aunt Lady Rose Bowes-Lyon, sister of the then Queen Elizabeth and wife of William Leveson-Gower, 4th Earl of Granville who was Northern Ireland's governor from 1945–52. The governor's position was abolished in 1973 and then direct rule from London came into force.

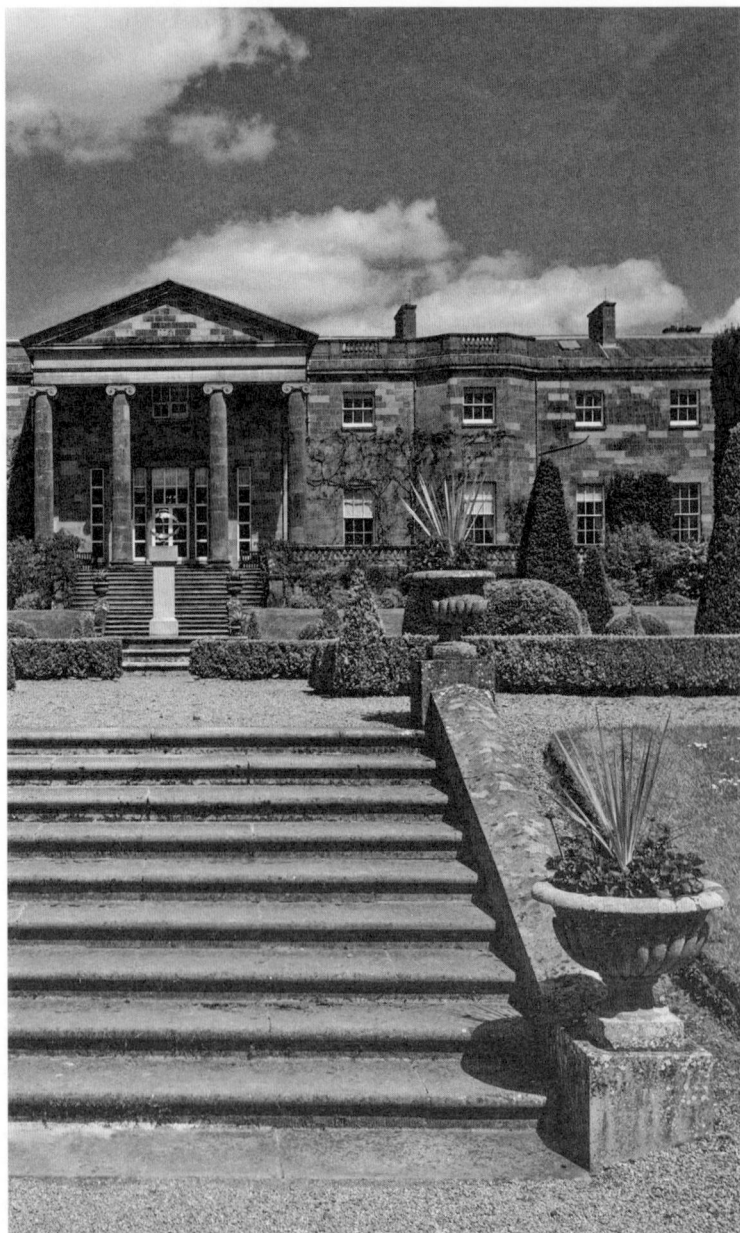

A tour of the house takes visitors through the elegant state rooms including the Throne Room – which doesn't have any thrones – and State Drawing Room. All have seen the rich and famous come through their doors including the Dalai Lama, the Crown Prince of Japan, Princess Diana, Hilary Clinton and Eleanor Roosevelt. Some of the rooms have hosted historic meetings between British and Irish politicians resulting in the castle playing an important role in the Northern Ireland Peace Process.

The table in the State Dining Room is set to let visitors see how royals might dine. Her Majesty sits with her back to the fire as the most senior diner. If you look carefully, you will see that the background on the Royal Coat of Arms above the fireplace is blue. Why not green, the true colour of Ireland? Well, in fact Ireland's true colour isn't green but blue, and the Irish Guards have blue plumes in their bearskins too. HRH the late Queen Mother sometimes wore blue to hand out shamrocks to them when she was Royal Colonel, a role now held by Prince William.

Visitors should be able to see the Chinese bowl which was valued when the Antiques Roadshow visited the castle some years ago. How much for? Ah, no one is privy to that information, but it is obviously worth a pretty penny.

During the 'Troubles' in the 1960s and 1970s security at Hillsborough was increased with the addition of bulletproof windows and a helipad to whisk important guests out and in more safely. This led to Hillsborough playing a key role in historic negotiations that would finally bring peace after 30 years. One secretary of state who was key to negotiations was Maureen 'Mo' Mowlem. She invited people to stay and managed to create a relaxed atmosphere that helped candid discussion. She adored the 100-acre gardens and sometimes, when official meetings became heated, she would take people outside to continue the talks in the more private, calming atmosphere. She loved the gardens so much some of her ashes were scattered here after her death in 2005. The gardens are a mix of ornamental grounds, woodland and a lake with interesting embellishments including a statue of Ossian, Lady Alice's Temple and an Ice House.

In 2014, Historic Royal Palaces took over the running of Hillsborough Castle.

Interesting facts about Hillsborough Castle:

• Viewed by some as a politically neutral venue, Hillsborough has played a role in the Northern Ireland Peace Process since the 1980s and negotiations for the Good Friday Agreement were conducted here in 1998.

• HM The Queen and HRH Prince Philip came here in July 1953. The Queen wore the Girls of Britain and Ireland tiara made for her grandmother Queen Mary and it is noted that strawberries and meringue were on the menu.

• The 3rd and 4th Marquesses commissioned much work on the house so its exterior nowadays looks much the same today as it was then.

Address: Hillsborough Castle, The Square, Hillsborough, BT26 6AG, Co. Down

Website: www.hrp.org.uk/hillsborough-castle

Visitor information: There are daily tours of the castle and gardens. At time of writing, the courtyard area at the lower end of the estate is being redeveloped into a multifunctioning space with café, shop, visitor information, ticketing and meeting spaces for visitors, schools and groups arriving by car and coach. Some discoveries have been made in this area, including the remains of early 18th-century pineapple houses and original hot house walls.

– SCOTLAND –

BALMORAL CASTLE, ABERDEENSHIRE

Prince Albert bought the castle and estate for his wife, Queen Victoria, in 1852 because she adored Scotland. Since then it has been the private property of the British royal family.

They say it's all about location, and this castle has bagsied one of the best. It stands 926 feet above sea level and commands glorious views far and wide. Dramatic mountain ranges, heather-clad hills, ancient Caledonian pine forests and the swift and clear River Dee; it's true, the magnificent scenery of Royal Deeside can't be upstaged.

Originally King Robert II of Scotland (1316–90) had a hunting lodge here known as Kindrochit. Later historical records show that a house at Balmoral was built by Sir William Drummond in 1390. The estate is recorded in 1451 as 'Bouchmorale' and after that was tenanted by Alexander Gordon, second son of the 1st Earl of Huntly. The Gordon family stayed with the castle until 1847, when Sir Robert Gordon died.

Since Victoria and Albert both loved Scotland – the landscape reminded Albert of Thuringia, his home in

Germany – he acquired the remaining part of the lease on Balmoral in 1848. This included furniture and staff. It could be said that they were taking a bit of a risk as neither he nor the Queen had seen the castle, and it wasn't until later that year that they made their first visit. Victoria wrote that the house was 'small but pretty' and that 'all seemed to breathe freedom and peace, and to make one forget the world and its sad turmoils'. In 1852 they bought it for £30,000 and then, because it was deemed too small for the royal couple's growing family, work began on their new home.

Construction began in 1853 on a site 100 yards north-west of the original building, so that the royal family could continue to occupy it while the new castle was being built. Their new home, the one that is still there today, was finished in 1856 at a cost of £100,000. When the new castle, made from local granite in Scottish baronial style, was complete, the old one was knocked down.

The royals often spent their summer and early autumn months here and following the death of Prince Albert, Victoria spent up to four months at a time at the castle. Other houses were then built in the grounds. There was the Garden Cottage for her children, Karim Cottage for her Indian Secretary the Munshi Abdul Karim and Baile-na-Coille for John Brown, her ghillie and manservant.

And speaking of John Brown, described by the Queen as her 'heart's best treasure', theirs was a relationship earning Victoria the nickname Mrs Brown. A 1997 film of the same name starred Dame Judi Dench and Billy Connolly.

John Brown was seven years younger than the Queen and started work at Balmoral in 1848. One day in 1863, two years after Albert's death, while out riding with two of her daughters, Victoria had a fall from her horse. She spent the next few days in bed with raw meat on her black eye. She

Photo: Chris Brown

had also hurt her neck and sprained her thumb. Her doctor told her she was able to keep on riding and from then on she depended on John Brown to accompany her. She wrote in her diary: 'A stranger would make me nervous. I am now very dependent on those I am accustomed to and in whom I have confidence.' Soon after that, Brown was given the title of the Queen's Highland Servant. Victoria wrote: 'He is so devoted to me – so simple, so intelligent, so unlike an ordinary servant, and so cheerful and attentive.' He treated her as an ordinary woman, not as a queen.

After he died in 1883, Victoria, the Queen and Empress of India, mourned him until she herself died in 1901. A bronze statue of John Brown stands at Balmoral. Victoria was buried with a gold wedding ring that had belonged to Brown's mother, which she wore constantly after his death. Also buried with her was a leather case containing a photograph of John Brown with locks of his hair, while other photographs of him, which she would carry in her pocket, were placed in her hand.

Queen Victoria described Balmoral as 'my dear paradise in the Highlands', though not everyone thought so highly of it. Disraeli disliked it, ex-British Prime Minister Tony Blair once called it 'freaky', Lady Dalhousie said 'I never saw anything more uncomfortable and that I coveted less' while Prince Leopold had such an aversion to it he refused to go there at all – much to his mother Queen Victoria's annoyance. However, brownie points go to the present queen's granddaughter, Princess Eugenie, who described it as 'the most beautiful place in the world'.

Interesting facts about Balmoral Castle:

• Today the 50,000-acre estate passes down by inheritance

and is the private property of HM Queen Elizabeth II, who visits every summer.

• Queen Victoria's youngest granddaughter, Victoria Eugenie Julia Ena, was born at Balmoral Castle on 24 October 1887. The princess was the first member of the royal family to be born in Scotland since Charles I in 1600 and the first royal child ever to be born at Balmoral.

• Prince Philip proposed to HRH Princess Elizabeth (now HM Queen Elizabeth II) here.

Address: Balmoral Castle, Ballater, Aberdeenshire, AB35 5TB

Website: www.balmoralcastle.com

Visitor Information: Admission charges include access to the formal and vegetable gardens, exhibitions in the stable area and the Ballroom, the castle's largest room. Other rooms in the castle are not available to the public as these are Her Majesty Queen Elizabeth II's private rooms.

Safari tours of the estate and the old Caledonian pine forest are also available. Wildlife species which guests may see include birds of prey, red squirrels, red deer, red grouse, black grouse, snow bunting and salmon.

An audio handset tour is available in English, Dutch, French, German, Italian and Spanish and there is a gift shop and café on site.

Self-catering, dog-friendly holiday cottages are available on the estate, though these are not let out during the time the royals are in residence.

DUNVEGAN CASTLE, SKYE

Once bold and brave and still breathtakingly gorgeous, Dunvegan Castle has been the stronghold of the chiefs of Clan MacLeod for nearly 800 years.

This proud castle has survived clan battles, famine and all the social, political and economic changes that have befallen the Western Highlands and islands. If Dunvegan Castle walls could talk, the story would make a great movie.

The story goes that in the spring of 1498 the chief of Clan MacLeod was invited to lunch with King James V. Seated beneath a vaulted ceiling at the monarch's vast table, dazzled by the gleam of a thousand candles, the insecure rural chieftain fell to bragging about his own wealth: 'On our MacLeod estate, Your Highness, we have a table even grander than this *and* candles brighter *and* ceilings that are higher.'

Well, that was not a sensible thing to say, especially to a bigwig like King James who thought he was the bee's knees and better than everybody else. 'Okay,' he smirked knowingly, 'I'm going to come up to your castle then and see this MacLeod grandeur for myself.'

MacLeod must have been shocked, because his place was nowhere near as grand as the King's. Anyway, back in MacLeod country, he got together with some of his advisors and they had a brainstorming session. Suggestions were thrown around but then the canny chief had a jewel of an idea.

When King James arrived in due course, ready to put the chief to shame for his wild remarks, a magnificent feast had been laid out on the grassy summit of a flat-topped mountain now known as MacLeod's Table (*Healabhal Mhor*). The starry heavens were the ceiling and hundreds of clansmen dressed in their finery held torches aloft as candles for the chief's gargantuan table. Let's hope the weather held long enough for them to enjoy their meal, presumably it did, but in any case, the King was well impressed. Wasn't that a good idea?

There was, indeed, still is, a Fairy Flag in the castle, though little of it now remains. This sacred banner, believed to date from the 7th century, was said to bring success to the chief or his clan if unfurled in an emergency. Good stuff, except there is a downside in that the charm will only work three times and it has already been used twice to secure MacLeod victories in battle. The upside is there is little chance of a battle these days.

The flag's origin is a rather far-fetched story actually but legend goes that a MacLeod chieftain named Malcolm married a fairy woman and they had a son. However the fairy quickly grew homesick for her mystical home land. Malcolm, being a good guy and putting his wife's happiness before his own, walked with her to Annwn, land of the fairies, leaving the infant heir to the lands of Dunvegan. Malcolm came back home alone and upset, on the night there was to be a feast celebrating his son's birth.

The feast was grand, with platters of venison, duck and beef served to everyone. Pipers from Clan MacCrimmon played and there was plenty of dancing and carousing with ale flowing. Throughout this, the baby slept, watched over by a young nursemaid. He slept so soundly that she decided to join the party for a short time. However, after she left, the baby started to cry and magically his mother, in Annwn, heard him. 'How can I help him?' she thought, and quickly wove a blanket of green silken thread with tiny spots to comfort him. Suddenly, the castle was filled with fairy voices, singing about the gift which the child had been given. They

DUNVEGAN CASTLE, SKYE

Photo: Willem van de Poll

told of the magic of the blanket, and how when they faced danger, the MacLeods were to wave the flag to keep them from harm – but that it would only work three times, so if any MacLeod waved the flag for trivial reasons then they'd better watch out. Plus it could only be used if a year and one day had passed since the last use. Everything comes with conditions attached, even from the fairies.

Anyway, Malcolm locked the flag in an iron case and made sure that the key would only ever be held by the clan chieftain. No one else would ever have possession of the flag either. Centuries passed and the flag went unused, until MacLeod lands came under attack from Clan MacDonald. The MacDonalds outnumbered the MacLeods and it was a close run thing until the MacLeod chieftain remembered the legend of the fairy flag. He waved it, the MacDonalds fell back and the MacLeods managed to drive them away.

Years later a disease ran among the livestock of each clan. Serious stuff because without the herds there would be no food or income. For the second time a MacLeod chieftain thought 'I'll try the flag' and waved it hoping that it would work. Yes, you're right, the sick cattle recovered and the disease vanished.

Another of the castle's treasures dates back to time of the 15th Chief, Sir Rory Mor, who was knighted by James VI. In 1596, Sir Rory was presented with the Dunvegan Cup, a gift from the O'Neills of Ulster as a token of thanks for supporting the cause against England. An inscription in Latin on its silver rim states: 'Katherine, daughter of King Neill, wife of MacGuire Prince of Fermanagh had me made in the year of God 1493.' Besides the Dunvegan Cup another heirloom which can still be seen today is Sir Rory Mor's Horn, a drinking horn. Tradition has it that the chief's heir, on coming of age, must take a full horn of claret and drain it in one gulp. No mean feat since the horn holds a bottle and a half!

In 1956, Her Majesty Queen Elizabeth II and HRH Prince Philip visited Dunvegan Castle. John, maternal grandson of the clan chief Dame Flora MacLeod of MacLeod, was challenged to quaff the horn which was filled with claret, and he did it in one minute 57 seconds. He must have been away with the fairies after that …

Interesting facts about Dunvegan Castle:

• Stoutly built, Dunvegan is possibly the oldest inhabited castle in Britain and today descendants of the MacLeods, the first owners, still live in it.

• The castle has starred in several films including *Highlander* (1986), *Macbeth* (2015) and *Made of Honor* (2008).

• The motto of Clan MacLeod is 'Hold Fast' and it is emblazoned above the bull's head on the MacLeod crest.

Address: Dunvegan Castle, Dunvegan, Isle of Skye, IV55 8WF

Website: www.dunvegancastle.com

Visitor information: There are regular guided tours of the castle and/or gardens. Seal-watching boat trips are also available on the loch, as are wildlife cruises. We know that Bonnie Prince Charlie left the Isle of Skye in a hurry, but you can stay for as long as you like when you come and where better to stay than in one of the four self-catering holiday cottages at the castle?

EDINBURGH CASTLE, EDINBURGH

The majestic, look-at-me castle, Scotland's number one visitor attraction, is perched on an extinct volcano at the top of the Royal Mile.

Dominating the skyline, this powerful national symbol of Scotland has seen many sieges throughout the centuries and today is a mix of military barracks, palace, fortress, war memorial and World Heritage Site.

Rich in history, the castle is home to the ancient Stone of Destiny, on which Scottish monarchs were crowned. That is, until Edward I of England, 'Hammer of the Scots' invaded Scotland in 1296 and took the stone from Scone (pronounced 'Scoon') near Perth to London where he had it built into his own throne. Since then it has been used in coronation ceremonies for monarchs of England and then Great Britain. In 1996, on St Andrew's Day, 30 November, Her Majesty Queen Elizabeth II allowed the stone to be returned to Scotland after 700 years. It is now in Edinburgh Castle Crown Room, alongside the Scottish Crown Jewels, known as the 'Honours of Scotland'. These are the oldest Crown Jewels in the British Isles and were first used in the coronation of Mary, Queen of Scots in 1543.

The oldest part of the castle is the beautiful though small St Margaret's Chapel, built in the 1100s to commemorate Margaret, King David's mother, who died here in 1093. An example of Romanesque architecture, this Category A-listed building was used by the royals as a private place of prayer up until the 16th century, when it was used to store gunpowder, before being restored as a chapel in 1845.

Due to the political situation at the time, the chapel was for many months the resting place of Mary of Guise, Regent of Scotland, who wanted Scotland to be Catholic and independent of England. Mary, mother to Mary, Queen of Scots, died on 11 June 1560. On 6 July, the French, Scots and English signed the Treaty of Edinburgh, agreeing that foreign soldiers, French and English alike, would withdraw from Scotland and in August the Scottish parliament passed legislation making the country officially Protestant. Not until the following year was permission given for Mary of Guise's burial and in March 1561 she was secretly carried from the castle in the dead of night and shipped to France. Although her remains rest in Reims, there are stories that her ghost haunts Edinburgh Castle.

Displayed on a terrace in front of St Margaret's Chapel is mighty Mons Meg, a 15th-century siege cannon, a gift from the Duke of Burgundy to James II. Her last shot was fired in October 1681. In the early days, the cannon was simply known as 'Mons' after the Belgian town of its origin. Unfortunately, her barrel burst and several years after that Mons was taken to the Tower of London, a casualty of the Disarming Act that demilitarised Scotland after the Jacobite Risings. She must have had a guardian angel because instead of being melted down, she was returned to Scotland 70 years later to be deposited at the port of Leith. Then, in a blaze of glory on 9 March 1829, she was accompanied by a military escort to her rightful place on the battlements of Edinburgh Castle. This most remarkable of all medieval guns had come home.

Meg isn't to be confused with the One o'clock Gun though, established as a time signal for ships. The gun fires from the ramparts every day, causing surprise and alarm to those pedestrians on Princes Street below who are unaware of the

Photo: Remi Mathis

ritual. If you happen to be there at this time of day, don't say I didn't warn you – and mind your ear drums. In April 1916 the gun was fired in anger when a German Zeppelin attacked Edinburgh, dropping bombs on the Castle Rock. The gun, apparently, frightened it off.

If you visit the castle and are an animal-lover like me, do take time to visit the Dog Cemetery, which since the 1840s has been a burial place for regimental mascots and officers' pets. Among the dogs buried here is Jess, band pet of the 42nd Royal Highlanders, more commonly known as the Black Watch, who died in 1881 and Dobbler, who travelled around the world with the Argyll and Sutherland Highlanders until he died in 1893.

The castle vaults below the Great Hall, which bristles with spears, swords and guns, have had many uses, not least as a prison. Their busiest period was during the War of American Independence between 1775 and 1783 and again during the wars with Revolutionary and Napoleonic France from 1793 to 1815. Among the prisoners was a five-year-old drummer boy taken at Trafalgar. In 1720 the vaults held 21 pirates whose ship was found full of Portuguese and French gold. They were found guilty and hanged below the high-water mark at Leith.

The castle esplanade is the home of the annual world-famous Edinburgh Military Tattoo, an event steeped in tradition which stirs the hearts of all who see it, whether or not they are Scottish. This unique event draws performers from all over the world with massed pipes and drums, military bands, display teams, dancers and the haunting lament of the Lone Piper set against the magnificent backdrop of Edinburgh Castle. The event, which began in 1950, hosts an audience of almost 9,000 people for each show.

Interesting facts about Edinburgh Castle:

• In ancient times the castle was called Dun Eidyn which means the 'stronghold of Eidyn'. When the Angles invaded in around AD 638, the rock began to be known by its English name of Edinburgh.

• An account of the first firing of the One o'clock Gun on 7 June 1861 (after two failed attempts) read: 'The third day the gun boomed out at one o'clock exactly, frightening the citizens and scattering the flocks of pigeons roosting on the city's buildings.'

• Prior to 1753, when the castle esplanade became a parade ground, it had a far more sombre use. At that time the open ground was an execution site and those accused of witchcraft or other dire deeds were burned at the stake.

Address: Edinburgh Castle, Castlehill, Edinburgh, EH1 2NG

Website: www.edinburghcastle.scot

Visitor information: The castle is open daily for guided and audio tours. A mobility vehicle is available for those unable to manage the castle's steep slopes. It transports visitors from the castle entrance to the highest point and back down at the end of the visit. Those who require this service, should ask a member of staff to arrange this on arrival. There are also a limited number of wheelchairs available.

EILEAN DONAN CASTLE, KYLE OF LOCHALSH

In an impossibly romantic setting, at the point where three sea lochs meet, picturesque Eilean Donan Castle is connected to the mainland by a stone bridge. It takes its name from the island on which it stands.

Representing the essence of a Scottish castle, this is one of the nation's most photographed. It appears on more calendars than any other and if you've seen a picture of a brooding Highland castle on a tin of shortbread, it will probably be this one.

The first fortified structure was built on the island in the early 13th century as a defensive measure, protecting the lands of Kintail against marauding Vikings who burst across the sea and started to control much of the north of Scotland and the Western Isles between 800 and 1266.

From the middle of that same century, this area was the Sea Kingdom of the Lord of the Isles because the sea was the main highway. At that time, the power of feuding clan chiefs was decided by the number of men and galleys or *birlinns* at their disposal. Eilean Donan offered the perfect defensive position. With its soaring towers and curtain wall, the castle encompassed almost the whole island.

By the 16th century a hornwork – a structure enclosing a courtyard and providing a more securely defended entrance – was added to the east wall, offering a firing platform for cannons. That was a handy ploy for the warring activities that would follow.

Eilean Donan played a role in the Jacobite Risings which ultimately culminated in the castle's destruction. In 1719 Jacobite William MacKenzie, the Earl of Seaforth, had the castle garrisoned by 46 Spanish marines who were supporting the Jacobites. The intention was to launch a second Armada and a main force would land in the South of England. Prior to that there would be an attack in north-west Scotland to divert attention. It was hoped the Scottish attack would raise Jacobite clans and lead government forces away from the site of the main landings. They had established a magazine of gunpowder and were awaiting delivery of weapons and cannon by sea. However, the main Spanish fleet carrying 7,000 men ran into a storm in the English Channel and was dispersed, causing their attack to be called off.

Anyway, the English government found out about the intended uprising and immediately dispatched three armed Royal Navy frigates: the Flamborough, the Worcester and the Enterprise, to subdue matters. They sailed into Loch Alsh and Loch Duich and bombarded Eilean Donan Castle for three days, though they only had limited success due to the strength of the castle walls – in some places they are fourteen feet thick. Captain Herdman of the Enterprise decided the only thing to do was to send his men ashore. It didn't take them long to overwhelm the Spanish defenders. The garrison surrendered and government troops blew up what remained of the castle to prevent it being used again, along with barrels of Spanish gunpowder which were stored inside.

Eilean Donan Castle was no more ...

... or was it? For the best part of 200 years, the stark ruins of Eilean Donan lay neglected, abandoned and open to the elements. Then Lt Colonel John Macrae-Gilstrap bought the island and along with his clerk of works, Farquhar Macrae, dedicated the following years to reconstructing glorious Eilean Donan. The plan of the castle was seen in a vision by Farquhar Macrae, which was confirmed years later when the original plans were found in Edinburgh.

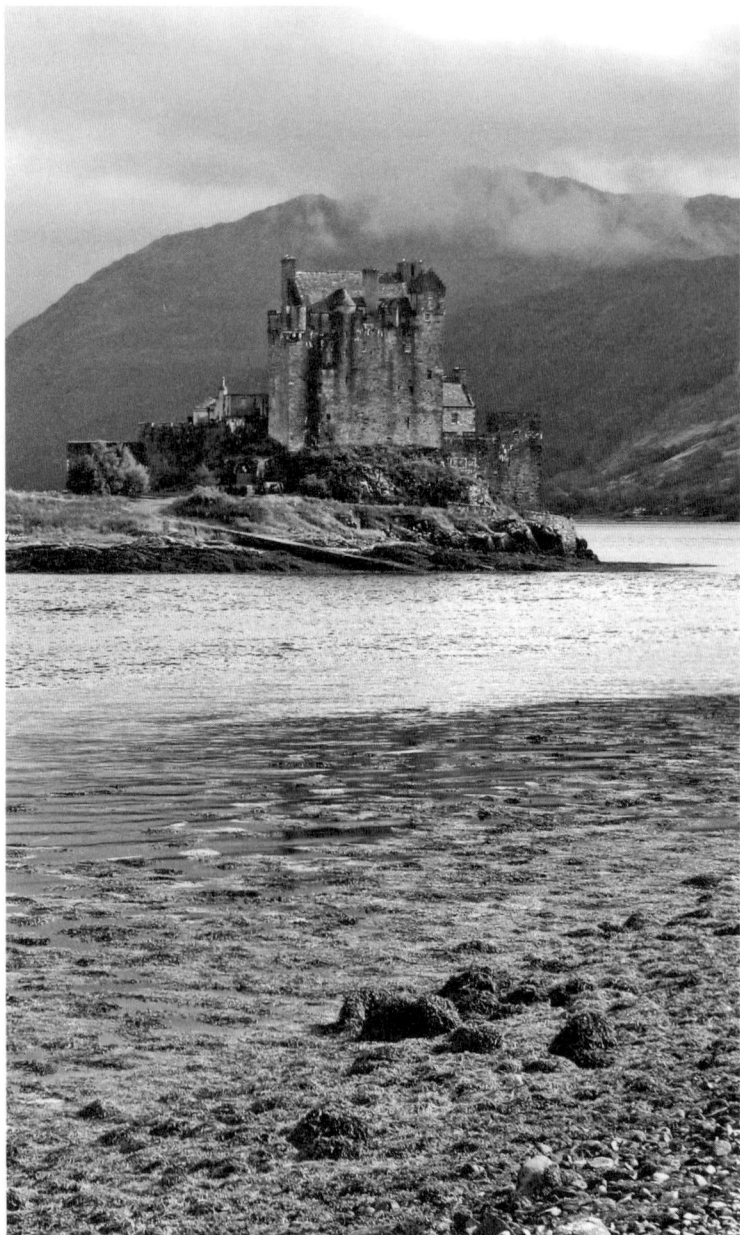

Photo: © Gilly Pickup

In 1912 rebuilding of the castle started and it was formally completed, restored to its full glory, in July 1932. It cost a quarter of a million pounds.

The story turns full circle and once again, this beautiful castle, headquarters of Clan Macrae, stands tall and proud against one of the world's most beautiful backdrops. The island is also home to the war memorial to members of the Clan Macrae who died in the First World War.

Interesting facts about Eilean Donan Castle:

• Alongside a selection of fine furniture in the banqueting hall, there is a fragment of tartan which belonged to Bonnie Prince Charlie, a lock of James III's hair and a sword which belonged to John Macrae.

• In 1331 the Earl of Moray hung sixteen Mackenzie heads on the walls after he executed them for law breaking.

• The castle is a popular location for films, advertisements, fashion shoots and music videos. It is the star of TV shows including *Highlander* (1992–8) and *The New Avengers* (1976–7), and films including *Bonnie Prince Charlie* starring David Niven in 1948, *Loch Ness* in 1996 and it was the Scottish headquarters of MI6 in 1999 Bond film, *The World is Not Enough*. There's no getting away from it, the sight of this glorious pile will certainly leave you less shaken, more stirred.

Address: Eilean Donan Castle, Dornie, Kyle of Lochalsh, IV40 8DX

Website: www.eileandonancastle.com

Visitor's information: The castle is open to the public from February to December and there is a visitor centre, gift shop and coffee shop on the premises. The Great Hall or Banqueting Hall is a magnificent room and a popular venue for weddings. Visitors can explore lots of rooms in the castle as well as visit a small museum and view displays in the recreated kitchens.

GLAMIS CASTLE, ANGUS

Almost Disneyesque in appearance, with towers galore and witch-hat turrets, Glamis Castle, childhood home of Elizabeth Bowes-Lyon, better known as HM Queen Elizabeth, the Queen Mother, is the ancestral seat of the Earls of Strathmore and Kinghorne.

Glamis Castle lies between the Sidlaw Hills and Grampian Mountains in the county of Angus in Scotland's north east. It was the birthplace of HRH Queen Elizabeth II's sister, the late Princess Margaret.

Robert I, more often referred to as Robert the Bruce, generously presented the lands to the Bowes-Lyon family as a gift in 1372. Since that date the Bowes-Lyon family have lived at Glamis Castle in unbroken succession and today it is home to Simon Bowes-Lyon, 19th Earl of Strathmore and Kinghorne.

When she was about fourteen years old, Lady Elizabeth Bowes-Lyon helped nurse soldiers from the First World War. They were convalescing in the castle, part of which became an auxiliary hospital for military personnel. Visitors can see the Billiard Room, originally a library, where a photo shows a young Lady Elizabeth seated at the 19th-century Erard baby grand piano, one of the room's main features. The room, which also has over 2,000 books on display, is where recuperating soldiers would come to play snooker and there are still some marks on a table from when the men laid their cigarettes down while they played.

The drawing room, one of the most impressive rooms, has a barrel-vaulted early-17th century Italianate ceiling and is still used occasionally by the family. The Queen Mother's sitting room with its wing-backed armchairs and family photographs is still kept as it was when Elizabeth and her new husband the Duke of York visited between 1923 and 1939.

With its splendid tapestries and weaponry, the castle also has links to Shakespeare's chilling tragedy *Macbeth*. The protagonist begins the play as Thane of Glamis before murdering his way to power, killing King Duncan while he is asleep in bed. While there is just the vaguest chance that Shakespeare visited Glamis, it was not the setting of the historic events. The real Macbeth actually killed Duncan in battle near Elgin long before Glamis Castle existed. However, in honour of the connection, one of the oldest rooms in the castle is known as Duncan's Hall. Just as Macbeth was overcome by visions of the ghost of Banquo, so Glamis is said to be haunted by many ghosts, one of whom, a woman with no tongue, has been seen in the grounds and occasionally spotted looking out of a barred window, gesturing at her terrible injuries.

Another spectre, believed to be the ghost of Janet Douglas, Lady Glamis, haunts the castle's family chapel. The chapel seats 46 people, and to this day one seat is always kept empty for the Grey Lady. No mortal is allowed to sit in it. She was burned at the stake as a witch in 1537 on Castle Hill, Edinburgh, on charges of plotting to poison the King. It is more than likely that the charges were fabricated for political motives. Holding on to power and property in Scotland in those days depended a lot on backing the right factions in conflict, and above all else, staying on good terms with the monarch.

Janet's trouble began when her brother Archibald Douglas, 6th Earl of Angus, kidnapped his stepson James V when he was a child. When the said James gained power in 1528, he decided to take his revenge on the whole of his stepfather's family, including Archibald's sister, the aforementioned Janet, widow of John Lyon, 6th Lord Glamis.

Hence the witchcraft accusation. James seized Glamis Castle for the Crown and regularly stayed there. Worse still, although Janet's son John, 7th Lord Glamis, was only a child, he was also condemned to death by James V and held captive. He was only released and the (ransacked) castle returned to him, when James died in Falkland Palace in 1542.

Relief all round then when relations with the Crown were fully restored during Mary Queen of Scots' stay at Glamis Castle in 1562 on her way North to quell a rebellion. She was extremely friendly towards the family, maybe trying to make amends for her father's wickedness to Lady Janet.

But it's not only Janet's ghost that wafts through the draughty corridors. Just as scary is the ghost of a young black boy, a badly treated servant who has been hanging around for over 200 years. He is reputed to haunt a seat by the door of the Queen's bedroom.

Probably the most terrifying of all Glamis Castle's ghosts is that of Earl Beardie, the 4th Earl of Crawford, who stayed as a guest at the castle. One night after a heavy drinking session he wanted to play cards. However, it being a Sunday, no-one would play. No cards on the Sabbath. Beardie was annoyed and said, 'please yourselves, I'll play with the Devil himself if

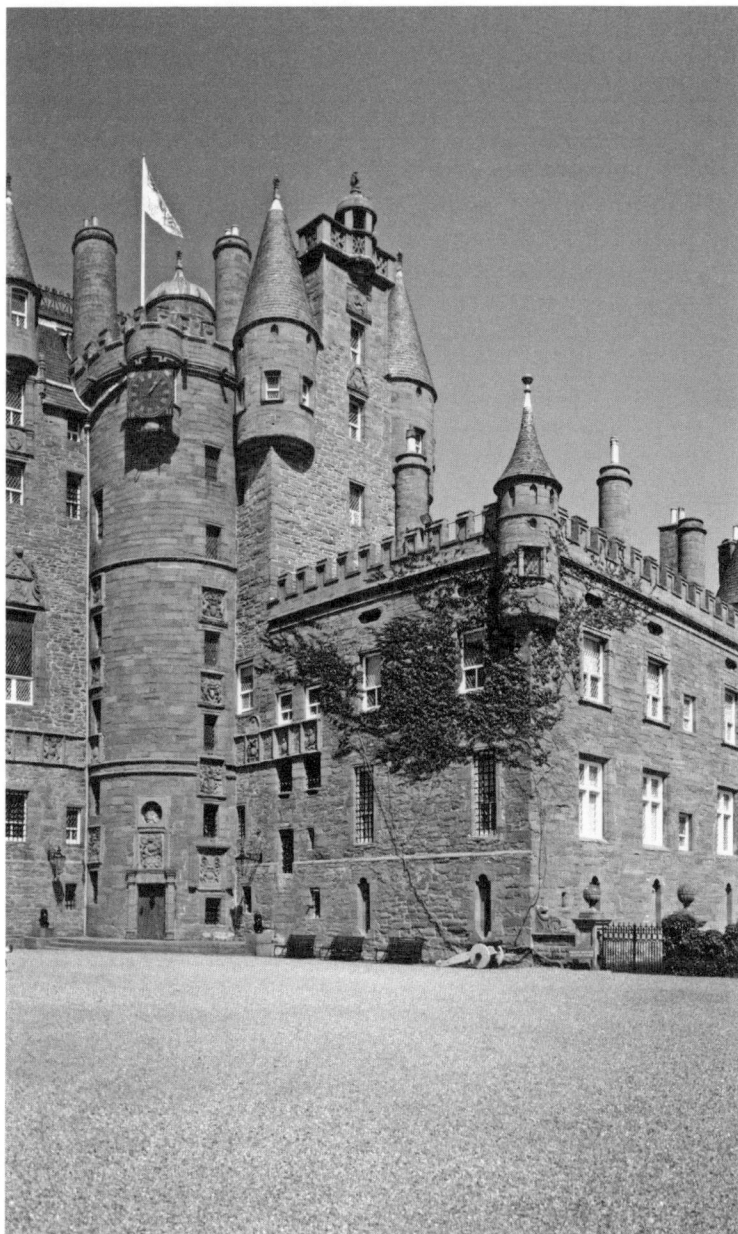

Photo: LeCardinal

I have to'. Just then, so the story goes – rather a coincidence it has to be said – a stranger arrived at the castle door asking Lord Beardie to play cards with him. Later servants heard shouting coming from the room. One peeped through the keyhole and the Earl burst from the room, angry with the servant for spying on him. When the servant returned to the room later, the stranger had disappeared and taken with him the Earl's soul, and so it is said Beardie has to play cards in that room for eternity.

Another strange thing linked to Earl Beardie happened at Glamis in 1486. A party of neighbouring aristocrats, the Ogilvies, showed up at the castle one day. They were desperate for help to protect them from their sworn enemies, the Lindsays, another local family, who had been threatening them will all sorts of nastiness. 'Of course,' said Lord Glamis, 'awa' an' come in', and escorted the Ogilvies to a chamber under the castle as a temporary safe haven. But – and here's the terrible thing – he locked them in the room and literally left them to starve to death! Why did he do that? Well, his good friend and drinking companion Alexander Lindsay, the 4th Earl of Crawford (Earl Beardie) was defeated by them during the Battle of Brechin in 1452.

Interesting facts about Glamis Castle:

• Lady Elizabeth Bowes-Lyon invited Prince Albert (later King George VI) to her home, Glamis Castle, though refused his marriage proposal twice before accepting.

• During the Civil War, Oliver Cromwell's men were billeted in the castle for a few months. They burned the furniture when they left so most pieces now date from 1650.

• There are 95 paintings in the chapel including a Jacob de Wet, dated 1688, depicting Christ disguised as a gardener wearing a hat.

Address: Glamis Castle, Angus, DD8 1RJ

Website: www.glamis-castle.co.uk

Visitor information: Parts of Glamis Castle – pronounced 'Glahms' – are open to the public. Public tours explore ten of the castle's 125 rooms. Regular events are held in the gardens.

PALACE OF HOLYROODHOUSE, EDINBURGH

The Palace of Holyroodhouse stands at the opposite end of the Royal Mile from Edinburgh Castle, against the spectacular backdrop of craggy Arthur's Seat, the tallest of Edinburgh's seven hills.

This grand pile, drenched in history and tapestries, is Her Majesty the Queen's official Scottish residence. During her Holyrood week, which usually runs from the end of June to the beginning of July, Her Majesty holds investitures in the Great Gallery, audiences in the Morning Drawing Room and a garden party, the largest annual event held at the Palace with around 8,000 guests. The Palace sits in ten acres, with the gardens covering eight of these.

The palace is fat with history so it is worthwhile taking a guided tour to relive the years when plotting, murder and all manner of goings on took place. One of its most famous residents was Mary, Queen of Scots, and this was the setting for some of the most dramatic episodes of her reign. The

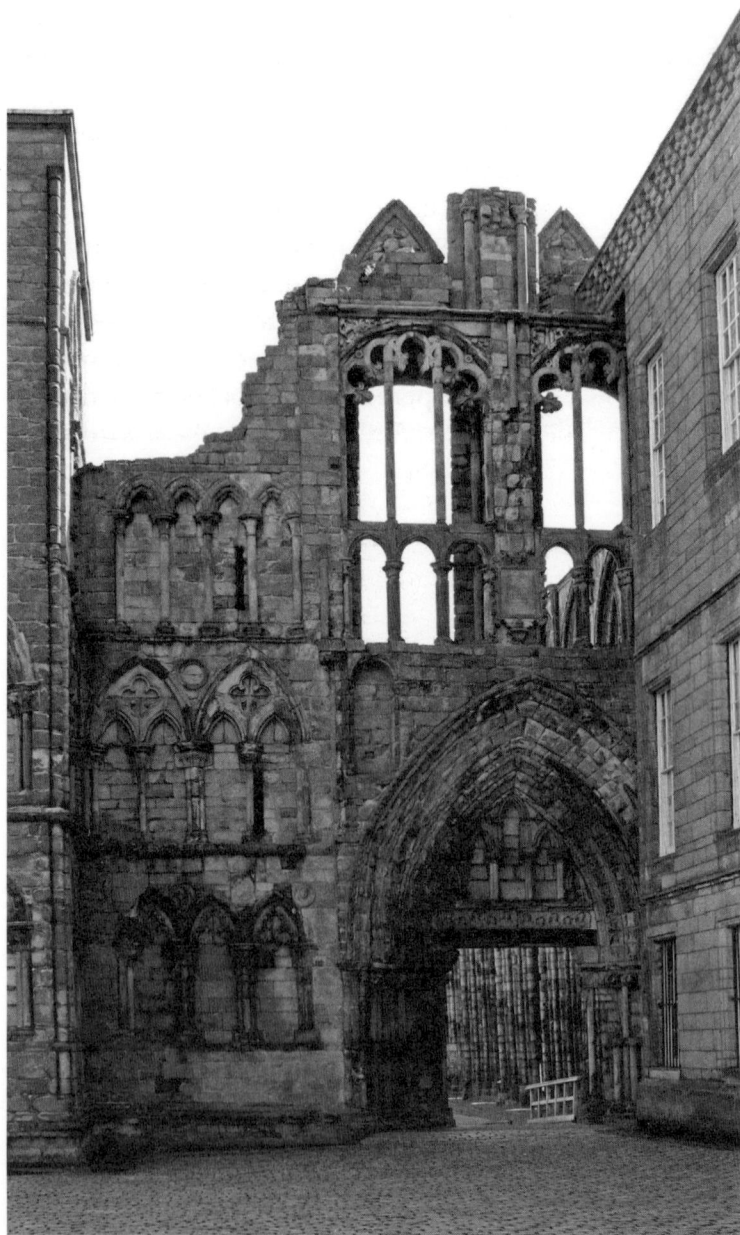

Photo: © Gilly Pickup

daughter of James V, Mary came to live at Holyroodhouse in 1561. She stayed in the James V Tower, built in 1528, the oldest part of the Palace.

It was here the 22-year-old Mary married her nineteen-year-old cousin, Henry Stuart, Lord Darnley on 29 July 1565. By marrying him, Mary thought she would strengthen the Catholic cause and enhance her claim to the English throne. Besides that, he was one of the few suitable men who was as tall as the five-foot-eleven Queen. It was after she nursed him through an attack of measles that she decided she'd marry him, saying he 'was the properest and best proportioned long man that ever she had seen'. At the wedding, she was dressed in '*deuil blanc*' – a black gown with white hood and veil to represent the widow's life she was leaving behind. When the ceremony was over, she threw off her mourning clothes and put on a brightly coloured, jewel-encrusted outfit. That was how they did things then.

One evening in 1566 when Mary was six months pregnant, she was eating supper in her private dining room with some friends and her Italian private secretary David Rizzio, who was an accomplished musician and singer. Darnley burst into the room with some Scottish nobles. Her husband had become increasingly jealous of the attention Mary paid to Rizzio and, encouraged by a group of Protestant nobles, decided that his wife and Rizzio were having an affair. Some say Darnley wanted to kill the baby she was carrying – the future James I and VI – because he wasn't certain if it was his or if it was Rizzio's. Mary realised the danger to Rizzio and shouted to the incomers: 'Leave our presence under pain of treason.' Lord Ruthven, who liked to dabble in black magic and who played an important role in the political intrigues of 16th-century Scotland, ignored her and told Darnley to seize Mary. Then a fight broke out and poor David Rizzio was dragged from the room to a tiny supper room and stabbed over and over again; 56 times in all. A plaque now marks the spot where he bled to death.

Queen Victoria first travelled to Scotland in 1842 and immediately fell in love with the country. This led to a change of fortunes for the Palace of Holyroodhouse, as it was considered a handy stopping off point on the journey North to Balmoral Castle. In her diary dated 3 September 1842 she wrote: 'We passed by Holyrood Chapel, which is old and full of interest, and Holyrood Palace, a royal-looking old place.'

The renovation of the somewhat dilapidated palace was supervised from London in preparation for the Queen's next visit and Holyroodhouse was reinstated as Scotland's primary royal residence. This brought the palace to the public's attention and inquisitive folks were keen to visit. Staff were on hand to show the 'Historical Apartments' with tickets costing sixpence each during the week, though on Saturdays visits were free.

A highlight for visitors is the Throne Room, used for receptions and state occasions. Queen Victoria had a new plaster ceiling installed in 1856 – she wanted to give the room greater dignity. However, Queen Mary described the ceiling as 'dreadful' so the room was altered again in 1929 when a new ceiling was installed to reflect the character of the Charles II original. A pair of thrones, commissioned by King George V in 1911, stand in the middle of the room. His ancestor, George IV visited Scotland in 1822, and was the first reigning British monarch to do so for around 200 years. In honour of the Scots, George IV had a Highland dress outfit specially made for his visit and he wore it to a grand reception in the Throne Room. His kilt was Royal Stewart tartan and he also wore traditional Highland weaponry, including a dirk (dagger), sword, belt and a powder horn, which is a container for gunpowder. These are all on display at the palace.

The State Apartments meanwhile have beautiful plasterwork ceilings and an unrivalled collection of French and Flemish tapestries. The rooms become progressively grander as you approach the King's Bedchamber, where only the most important guests would have been granted an audience. The Queen's Gallery, which opened in 2002 and is the newest addition to the palace, hosts a programme of changing exhibitions from the Royal Collection throughout the year.

The palace was selected as the site of the Scottish National Memorial to King Edward VII and his statue was unveiled by George V in 1922. Also around that time, improvements which included the installation of central heating and electricity were carried out and it was George V who gave the palace its status as the sovereign's official residence in Scotland.

Interesting facts about the Palace of Holyroodhouse (especially for those who like numbers):

• The palace has 289 rooms and the biggest is the Great Gallery. There are also a total of 387 windows and 51 clocks.

• There are 106 members of staff, although no one lives there, except for when the Queen is in residence.

• At the annual summer garden party with its 150-metre-long buffet table, 15,000 cups of tea are drunk as well as 42 gallons of iced tea. Nine thousand strawberry tarts and 7,000 sandwiches are consumed.

Address: Palace of Holyroodhouse, Canongate, Edinburgh EH8 8DX

Website:
www.royalcollection.org.uk/visit/palace-of-holyroodhouse

Visitor's information: The Palace is open to visitors from April to October. Check the website for opening times and prices. Disabled visitors pay a concessionary fee and are allowed to take in one companion free of charge.

STIRLING CASTLE, STIRLING

Murders, baptisms, sieges and a coronation – this beautiful castle has seen them all.

The royals who lived here – and over the centuries there were many, including the Stuart kings – didn't do things by halves. They were a showy lot with pockets as deep as Loch Ness. They enjoyed hunting in the forests around the castle, partied to the sounds of hurdy-gurdies and bagpipes, drank lots of punch – in those days it was thought to prevent tooth decay – held glittering balls, three-day long baptism ceremonies and tucked into enormous banquets.

Not that it was all fun. This castle was the scene of serious plottings, a murder and besides that, because it was a pretty important pile, it was besieged countless times including once by Cromwell's English troops in the 1650s.

At least that siege didn't last as long as one in 1304, when the castle was bombarded by lead balls stripped from nearby church roofs, stone balls and gunpowder mixture. It went on from April to July. Let's hope the folks inside had enough food, otherwise they must have been starving by the end. That was when King Edward I of England (the so-called 'Longshanks') was so desperate to take the castle that he arrived with seventeen trebuchets including his favourite, the 'war wolf'. For those who don't know what a trebuchet is, it is perhaps best described as a giant catapult.

Edward tried hard to control Scotland, but didn't reckon on how tough Scots could be when their backs were to the wall. Not that this skirmish was a one-off. These wars, later called Scotland's Wars of Independence, lasted on and off for around half a century.

The castle's golden age was during the late 1400s and 1500s, when the Scottish courts of James IV and James V were based here. In 1452 there was a hiccup amid all the fun and carousing when James II murdered William, 8th Earl of Douglas with the help of his courtiers. In the frenzied attack, William was stabbed 26 times and his body thrown from a window.

James II was still being grumpy in 1457 when in an effort to try to encourage his subjects to practice military skills, in particular archery, he decreed that 'futeball and golfe be utterly cried down', though his wish was ignored by almost everybody.

Both James IV and James V enlarged and developed the castle, creating a royal Renaissance complex of buildings, the likes of which had never been seen before in Scotland.

Mary Queen of Scots, daughter of James V and Marie de Guise, was crowned here aged nine months on 9 September 1543. In due course, her son, the future King James VI was baptised here in a glittering three-day ceremony. Festivities included a mock medieval tournament, a lavish banquet with an Arthurian theme, the allegorical siege of an enchanted castle on the open ground in front of the castle and Scotland's first firework display. Mary, who was a bit of a show-off, was determined to make the point that Scotland could rival the most ambitious celebrations to be seen at any European court, even if she had to borrow from the merchants of Edinburgh to pay for it.

Not that everything during the proceedings was perfect. Mary refused to let the Archbishop of St Andrews, whom she referred to as 'a pocky priest', spit in the child's mouth, as was then the custom. You can't blame her. The Godmother, Queen Elizabeth I, didn't turn up, though she sent a gold font and a representative who remained outside in protest of the Catholic ceremony. To top it all, dim, immature Lord Darnley, the child's father, sulked throughout proceedings because rascally, rebellious blue-eyed Bothwell had so clearly become the beautiful, witty Queen's favourite that it was he who received the guests at the ceremony.

It has to be said that situation didn't please the Scottish lords or John Knox, who named her the 'Scottish whore'. Nevertheless it was an ultra-lavish ceremony. These royals certainly had money to burn. Speaking of burning, the castle was cold, despite the huge fires. In 1567 Mary Queen of Scots wrote that the castle was 'damp and cold' and was worried because baby James 'was in danger of catching rheumatism'.

After baby James grew up and got married, he chose to have his own son Henry christened here too, in 1594. But he went one better than his mum did as far as celebrations went. He organised a fantastic display in the Grand Hall, which included a huge wooden ship with 40-foot-high masts. The ship was stuffed with seafood for the guests' dinner. The ship also had 36 brass cannons that fired a salute to the

Photo: © Gilly Pickup

baby prince. Besides the fish, there was a splendid banquet, plays and tilting to entertain guests and a shower of gold and silver coins were thrown out of windows for the common people to catch.

However it all went sour when James VI hightailed it to England in 1603 to take up his role as King James I of England. He made a promise to return to Scotland every three years. In fact he returned just once in the 22 years until his death.

His entry into London was triumphant. Members of the nobility travelled to London to witness the event. After it was over James wrote: 'The people of all sorts rode and ran, nay, rather flew to meet me, their eyes flaming nothing but sparkles of affection, their mouths and tongues uttering nothing but sounds of joy, their hands, feet, and all the rest of their members in their gestures discovering a passionate longing and earnestness to meet and embrace their new sovereign.'

But James, a Scot through and through, had something of an odd relationship with the English. After the Gunpowder Plot, the majority of the English were sympathetic to him but he kept them at bay. James didn't understand that English people wanted to see their king. Once, when told by a courtier that the public wanted to see his face, James replied, 'God's wounds! I will pull down my breeches and they shall see my arse!'

After James' departure, Stirling Castle's purpose swiftly changed from swanky royal home to military base. The Great Hall became a stable and cart shed – what a come down – and was damaged during the siege (yes, another one), by General Monck in 1650. The castle last saw military action in the Jacobite Rising of 1745 when troops besieged poor Stirling Castle.

On the plus side though, it was the last siege of a castle anywhere in Britain.

Interesting facts about Stirling Castle:

• Although Mary, Queen of Scots' family name was spelled 'Stewart', during her time in France she adopted the French spelling of 'Stuart', there being no 'w' in the French alphabet at the time.

• In 1507, Italian alchemist John Damian was in attendance at James IV's court. He thought that if he wore feathered wings, he would be able to fly so jumped from the battlements. Needless to say it didn't work and John landed in a dunghill breaking his thigh.

• Mary, Queen of Scots enjoyed sports and liked football. Behind the panelling in the queen's chamber, the oldest surviving football in the world was discovered. No one knows for sure, but the story is that she hid it in a safe place to protect it from witchcraft. The ball, made from an inflated pig's bladder is wrapped with cow hide and is around half the size of today's footballs.

Address: Stirling Castle, Castle Esplanade, Stirling, FK8 1EJ

Website: www.stirlingcastle.scot

Visitor information: The castle is open daily for guided tours and audio guides are available in six languages. There are gift shops and a café on site.

– WALES –

CAERNARFON CASTLE, CAERNARFON

The small fishing town of Caernarfon is hugged within Caernarfon Castle's mighty stone walls.

The UNESCO World Heritage Site of Caernarfon (English spelling: Caernarvon) is enshrined in myth and legend. One recounts the dream of a Roman emperor, in which he travelled to a faraway place where he saw a wonderful, multicoloured castle. After his dream, he sent messengers all over the world to try to find this must-have building. It was identified in Caernarfon.

King Edward I, an ambitious sort, had illusions of grandeur and the thought of building his chief Welsh residence on the spot enshrined in Roman mythology greatly appealed to him.

Inspired by legends and also by the Roman city of Constantinople with its vast walls, colour-banded masonry and octagonal towers, he chose to build a castle like no other in Caernarfon.

So in due course, he built the castle and walled town as part of his bid to encompass the Kingdom of Gwynedd (North Wales) within a chain of fortifications. He wanted to create a nucleus of English influence in this area of Wales and intended the castle to be not only a fortress and royal palace, but also the seat of government from which his descendants would rule the principality. Incidentally, a significant number of Welsh castles, including Caernarfon, can be described as concentric castles. They all encompass some or all of the following elements – a round keep, a stronger central keep or main tower, a high wall, at least one lower, outer wall surrounding the inner high wall and a drawbridge and moat.

Edward I also built Harlech, Beaumaris and Conwy Castles, but Caernarfon Castle was his most impressive, with walls that seemingly go on forever and providing pretty much everything his upmarket visitors would have required. It cost a pretty penny, a gasp-inducing £22,000, much more than the Treasury's yearly income. However, if you're a monarch you can get away with things like that, or at least, you could back then.

An important feature of Caernarfon Castle is its access to the sea. During its construction, men, equipment and building materials were transported by boat to the site of the castle and hundreds of tradesmen came from near and far to work on it. Timber was shipped in from Liverpool, Anglesey and elsewhere in North Wales and labourers came from as far as London to work on the construction. But it wasn't just the ambition of Caernarfon which made it incredible, it was the fact it was built so quickly. Even although it was built by hand, it was substantially completed in just five years. In 1287 it was finished.

The advantages of swift and easy accessibility via the sea ensured that the new fortified town, which was built at the same time as the castle, became a successful and prosperous stronghold for its English inhabitants.

Caernarfon Castle is equipped with two mighty gatehouses. One is the King's Gate, the other the Queen's Gate, which faces seaward. The Queen's Gate's purpose was to receive supplies unloaded from ships and it was never completely finished. Nowadays it contains the museum of the Royal Welch Fusiliers.

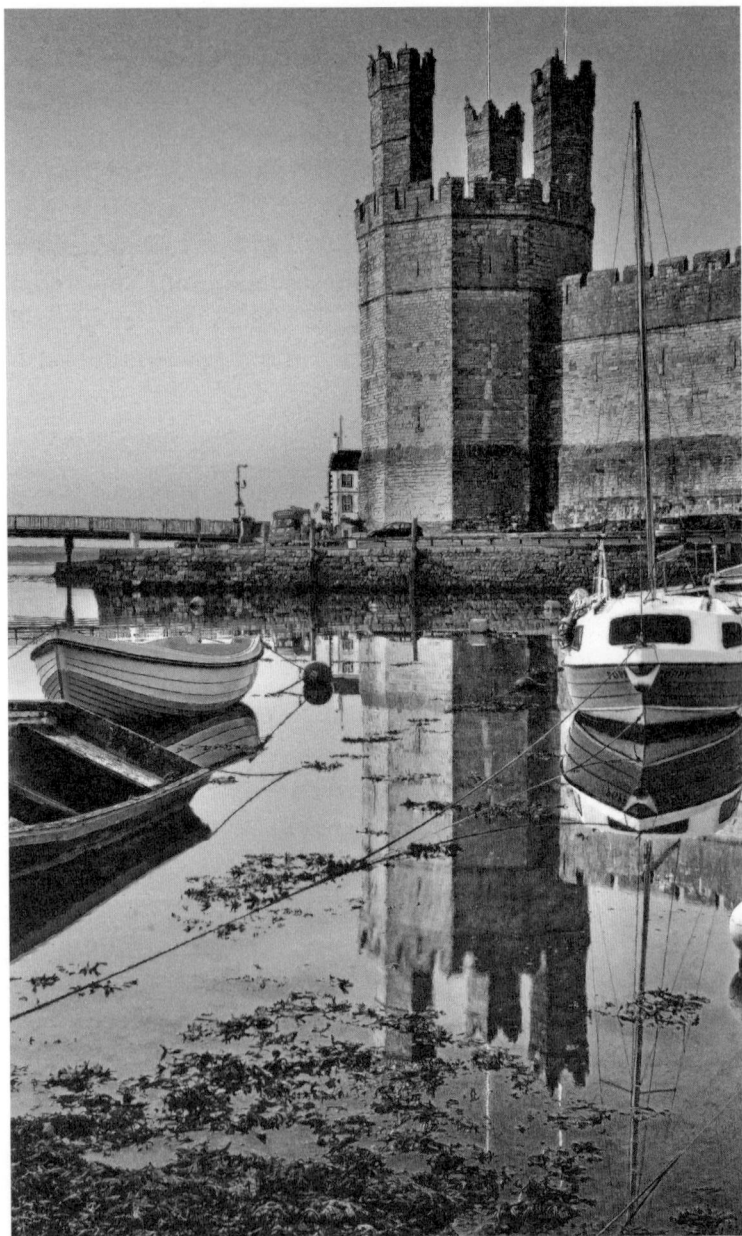

Photo: Richard Outram

As Edward's official residence, Caernarfon was an obvious site of discontent for Welsh rebels who weren't at all thrilled with the English domination of their native country. Consequently, it was the site of varied, increasingly ferocious attacks. The Welsh revolt of 1294 caught the English off guard. The uprising against English rule was led by Madog ap Llywelyn, and destroyed much of Caernarfon's town walls. They even managed to occupy the castle. Edward I mustered troops to quell the rebellion. In 1295, he recaptured Caernarfon, rebuilt destroyed walls and punished the Welsh for their revolt.

Interesting facts about Caernarfon Castle:

• The birth in 1284 of Edward I's son in the castle meant the child – Edward of Caernarfon – was legitimately Welsh and was crowned Prince of Wales in 1301. Since then, the eldest son of the sovereign has been granted the same title. In 1911, the future Edward VIII was invested at Caernarfon Castle and in 1969, the castle gained universal fame as the setting for the investiture of HRH Prince Charles as HRH Prince of Wales.

• Edward II was born on 25 April, two days after St George's Day. So instead of being born on the day of England's patron saint, he was born on St Mark's Day, then considered unlucky.

• Legend says the Druid wizard Merlin was born in a cave outside Caernarfon.

Address: Caernarfon Castle, Caernarfon, LL55 2AY

Website:
http://cadw.gov.wales/splash?orig=/daysout/caernarfon-castle

Visitor information: Caernarfon Castle is a major tourist attraction in Wales. Castle and grounds are open to the public with events taking place throughout the year. Admission is free for disabled visitors and a companion. Access to the castle is by way of two sets of steps, or a purpose-built access ramp. Wheelchair access is available throughout the lower level. Although Caernarfon Castle has been the property of the Crown since it was built, it is currently cared for by Cadw, the Welsh government's historic environment division, responsible for the maintenance of Wales' historic buildings.

CONWY CASTLE, CONWY

Conwy Castle in the medieval Welsh walled town of the same name was built by Edward I during his conquest of Wales and it played a significant role in several wars.

Brimful of history, tradition and splendid architecture, Conwy Castle was built between 1283 and 1287 for King Edward I. It was designed by master builder James of St George, an architect who designed many of Edward I's castles, including Harlech and Caernarfon and cost around £15,000 to build. That was a considerable sum at that time and was the most Edward spent in such a short time on any of his Welsh castles. It was probably worth it though because some say it is the most magnificent of the sovereign's Welsh fortresses.

Interesting to think that although now its stonework is

grey, in its heyday it would have been plastered with a white lime render. The dazzling white castle must have looked magnificent when approached by land or sea.

The heart of the castle is the Inner Ward, which contains the suite of apartments built for King Edward and Queen Eleanor*. Principal rooms were on the first floor, with heated though dark basements below. Two barbicans – fortified gateways – eight towers and a bow-shaped hall are contained in its distinctive elongated shape, due in part to the narrow rocky outcrop on which it stands. One thing that's different though, you won't find Edward's concentric 'walls within walls' here. They weren't needed because the rock base was enough security in itself.

In August 1399 Richard II took refuge here from the forces of Henry Bolingbroke, who later became better known as Henry IV. Two years later the castle was captured by supporters of Welsh independence fighter Owain Glyndŵr, who tricked their way in while the garrison was at prayer. Rhys ap Tudur and his brother Gwilym, cousins of Owain Glyndŵr, pretended to be castle carpenters and gained entry by killing the watchmen on duty to take control of the castle. When they were securely inside, Welsh rebels attacked and captured the rest of the town and burned most of it down. The independence fighters had control of the castle for three months and then they negotiated a surrender. They must have had good bargaining skills because Henry IV gave them ransom money and a royal pardon as part of the deal. They used the money to win back control of most of Wales and declare what was a short-lived independence from England.

Conwy Castle fell into disrepair by the early 17th century and Charles I sold it to Edward Conway, 1st Viscount Conway, in 1627 for £100. Edward's son, also called Edward, inherited what was by then essentially a ruin in 1631.

During the Civil War, Conwy Castle saw military action as it was held for the king by John Williams, Archbishop of York. In 1646 it was one of the last Royalist strongholds to surrender and in 1665 it was partially slighted – deliberate destruction so that the building is no use as a fortress – but the castle and town walls were left essentially intact.

At the end of the 18th century the castle was no more than a picturesque ruin which attracted visitors and artists including Thomas Girtin, J.M.W. Turner and Moses Griffith.

Nowadays the castle is among the finest surviving medieval fortifications in Britain and is a UNESCO-listed World Heritage Site.

Interesting facts about Conwy Castle:

• There is a great description of the castle in the guidebook published by CADW, the Welsh Historic Trust, which says, 'Conwy is by any standards one of the great fortresses of medieval Europe.'

• *In 1254, fifteen-year-old Edward travelled to Spain for an arranged marriage to Eleanor of Castile who was still only a child. Even though it may seem unlikely because of their young ages, theirs turned out to be a loving marriage. When Eleanor died in 1290 her body was ceremonially carried from Lincoln to Westminster for burial and a memorial cross was erected at each of the twelve resting places, including what became known as Charing Cross in London.

• The castle is sometimes called Conway Castle because it was owned by the Conway family intermittently throughout its history.

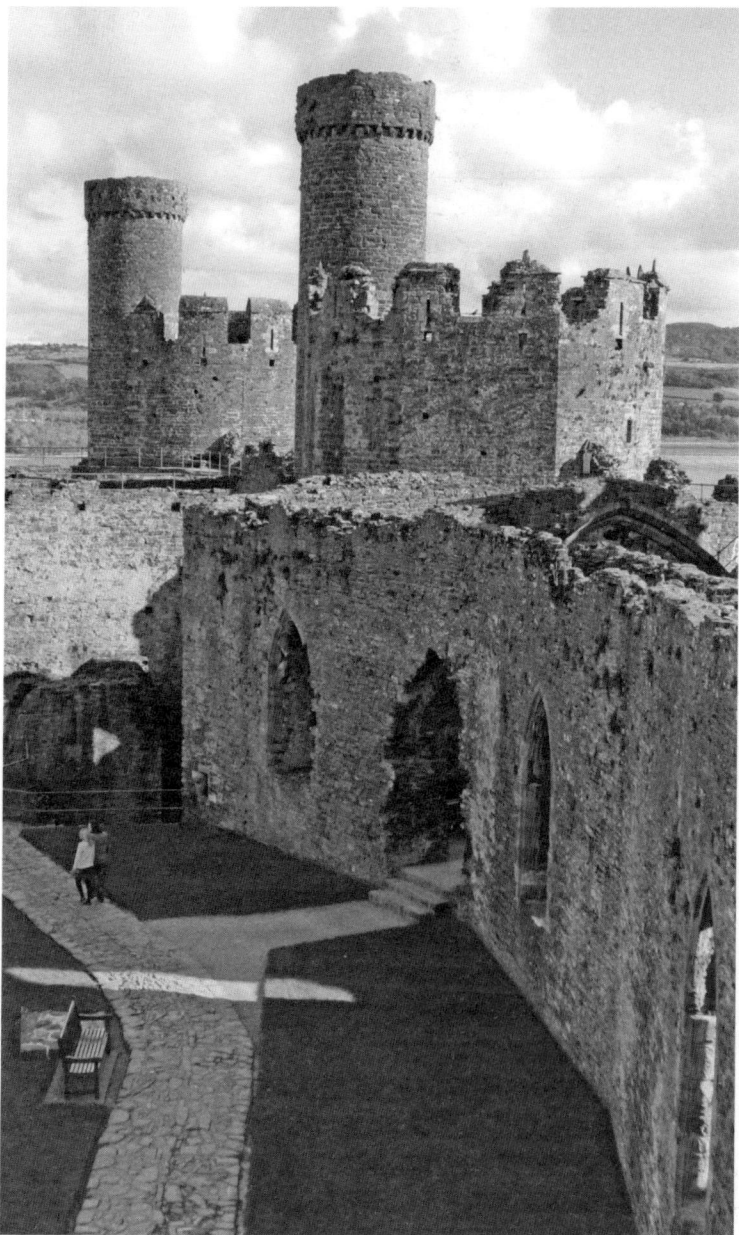

Photo: Robert Linsdell

Address: Conwy Castle, Rose Hill St, Conwy LL32 8AY

Website: http://cadw.gov.wales/daysout/conwycastle

Visitor information: The castle is open year-round. Disabled visitor and companion admitted free. The castle is on high ground with access from the visitor centre via timber road bridge and steep concrete ramp and steps. Wheelchairs restricted to visitor centre only.

More than 180,000 people a year visit Conwy Castle.

EUROPE

– AUSTRIA –

SCHÖNBRUNN PALACE, VIENNA

This Rococo palace was the summer retreat for Hapsburg emperors from the 1700s until 1918 and is Austria's most-visited site as well as Vienna's number one attraction.

Way back in the mid-13th century, the area around Schönbrunn belonged to the Klosterneuburg Monastery which still exists today. Austria's most prominent dynasty, the Habsburgs, acquired the land in 1569, originally using it as a hunting ground. Schönbrunn, which means 'beautiful spring', was named for a water source discovered by Emperor Matthias while hunting. The first mention of the name,

Schönbrunn, was in 1642. Before that the estate was called the Katterburg and had its own corn mill, arable farm and vineyards. The land stayed in Hapsburg hands until 1918.

In 1696 Emperor Leopold I commissioned architect Johann Bernhard Fischer von Erlach to design an imperial hunting lodge for his son, Crown Prince Joseph, who would later become Emperor Joseph I. Fischer von Erlach was one of the great architects of his time, a real high flyer, responsible for other look-at-me Viennese buildings including the Karlskirche, Palais Schwarzenberg and the Winter Stables for the Spanish Riding School. However, when he submitted his original plans they were dismissed as 'over ambitious'. He then went on to win the commission from Emperor Leopold for the next set he submitted.

It was some 40–50 years later that the palace attained its full glory, thanks to Empress Maria Theresia, the only female Habsburg ruler and mother of Marie Antoinette, one of Maria and Franz Stephan's sixteen children. Schönnbrunn was a wedding gift from her father and until the 23 year old's reign which began in 1740, it had only been used as an occasional summer retreat or dowager residence. Maria Theresia really liked it though, so much so that she made it her full-time summer residence. As she grew older she increasingly suffered from the effects of summer heat and in the last ten years of her life had a suite furnished for herself on the ground floor facing the gardens.

Speaking of gardens, the Great Parterre is the largest open space in the Palace grounds. In the mid-18th century the beds consisted of formal patterns created with strips of box hedging. These were known as *broderie parterres* since these motifs were mostly taken from embroidery patterns. At the time, the two larger sections of parterre enclosed what were called *boulingrins* derived from the English words

Photo: Thomas Wolf, www.foto-tw.de

'bowling green'. This sunken lawn was originally intended for games of bowls but in French horticultural design was used as a decorative element. The Orangery, commissioned by Emperor Franz I Stephan in 1754, is one of two of the world's longest baroque orangeries. It was also the setting for dazzling court festivities and Joseph II liked to organise banquets here.

Franz Joseph I Emperor of Austria and King of Hungary was born in Schönbrunn Palace in 1830. Extensive refurbishments and changes accompanied his accession in 1848 and his subsequent marriage to sixteen-year-old Elisabeth, daughter of Duke Maximillian Joseph of the House of Wittelsbach in 1854. The imperial couple were the only royals after Maria Theresia to make Schönbrunn their preferred summer residence though Elisabeth, known as 'Sisi' spent much of her time away from Vienna and the constraints of court life. When she first married she did not get on well with her bossy mother-in-law, Archduchess Sophie, who had the final say in the upbringing of Elisabeth's daughters. When the male heir, Rudolf, was born, things improved slightly but Elisabeth's health suffered under the strain and she often left Schönbrunn to visit Hungary where she felt more relaxed. It was sad that her life came to an abrupt, tragic end in 1898 though. When she was travelling in Geneva she was stabbed to death by Italian anarchist Luigi Lucheni. Sisi was the longest serving Empress of Austria, at 44 years.

When the imperial family left Schönbrunn after the First World War, palace staff retained rights to remain in their home. Efforts were made to turn the palace into a children's home and as somewhere to train nursery school teachers. Unfortunately, it quickly became obvious that the building was too expensive for them to heat and maintain.

After the end of the monarchy in 1918, Schönbrunn passed into state ownership. After the Second World War, British occupation forces used parts of Schönbrunn for administrative offices and the British military held parades and celebrations in the palace grounds.

The Austrians regard Schönbrunn Palace and its vast grounds as one of the most important historical and architectural monuments in the country. They are, after all, an intact example of baroque architecture and Schönbrunn is listed as a UNESCO World Heritage Site.

Interesting facts about Schönbrunn Palace:

• Six-year-old Wolfgang Amadeus Mozart impressed Empress Maria Theresia with his musical skills at Schönbrunn in 1772. He played duets with his older sister, Nannerl in the Mirror Room. Of the castle's 1441 rooms, this is the most famous with its white and gold Rococo decoration and crystal framed mirrors.

• Maria Theresia was said to be beautiful, especially when young. A Prussian emissary at the Vienna court described her as having a round face, slightly reddish blonde hair and pale blue eyes. Although he also said: 'After going through childbirth numerous times and filling out, she has become somewhat sluggish.'

• The Marie Antoinette Room served as a dining room. Now visitors can see the table laid as it would have been for a family dinner back in the day, with Viennese porcelain, silverware and prism-cut lead crystal glasses. Court dinners were ruled by the strictest etiquette and diners were allowed to converse softly only with their immediate neighbour.

Address: Schönbrunn Palace, Schönbrunner Schloßstraße 47, 1130, Vienna

Website: www.schoenbrunn.at

Visitor information: Around 3 million people visit Vienna's Schönbrunn Palace every year. The Imperial Tour allows visitors to see inside the apartments of Emperor Franz Joseph and his wife Sisi as well as the Great Gallery. Those interested in a more in-depth look at the history of the complex may choose the Grand Tour which allows access to 40 rooms open to the public. In the Herringbone Room visitors learn what everyday life was like at the imperial court. The Labyrinth offers games for all ages and has a giant kaleidoscope which allows visitors to see themselves from every angle. If they so wish, the more athletic can climb a chiming climbing pole and ring the bell at the top.

– BELGIUM –

ROYAL PALACE OF BRUSSELS, BRUSSELS

With a grandstand location in the centre of Brussels, the Royal Palace is the official residence of the royal family, although they haven't lived here for over 100 years.

Since 1831 the royal family have lived in the Royal Palace of Laeken, on the outskirts of the city, but the Royal Palace is where the king exercises his royal duties and welcomes guests of the state. Some government ministries are also located here.

There used to be a palace called Coudenberg on this spot. It had stood here since the Middle Ages and was the home of the various Dukes of Brabant who extended and improved it over the years. Unfortunately the building was wiped out by fire in 1731 and it wasn't until around a century later that it was finally rebuilt.

After the Belgian revolution when Belgium split from the Netherlands to become an independent country, the palace was offered to the German Prince Leopold of Saxe-Coburg when he became 1st King of the Belgians in 1831. He used it for receptions and official events but for some reason preferred to make the Royal Palace of Laeken his home. During his reign, which lasted until he died in 1865, nothing much was done to improve or extend the Royal Palace.

His son, the unpopular Leopold II, had a different view and soon got to work on embellishing and improving the building. It was much too modest for a king such as he, was his opinion. During his kingship, the palace almost doubled in size and the Grand Staircase, Throne Room and Grand Gallery were added. He decided that his new palace façade, built in 1904, would outshine that of Buckingham Palace in London, by making it half as long again.

The current king, King Philippe, is the 7th King of Belgium, born in 1960 at Laeken and educated at Trinity College, Oxford and Stanford University, California. He became king on 21 July 2013 after his father, King Albert II, abdicated due to ill health. Philippe is married to Countess Mathilde d'Udekem d'Acoz and they have four children. The eldest is Princess Elizabeth (now heir to the throne), who also has the title Duchess of Brabant. There is also Prince Gabriel, Prince Emmanuel and Princess Eléonore.

Photo: el legowo

In summer 1965 it was agreed that the palace would be open to the public, a tradition which has been followed each year since. Because it is still very much a functional government building and very much the king's place of work, it is open only during the summer, typically late July to mid-September, when much government business is on hold and the king and queen are on holiday. While not all rooms are open to the public there is still a lot for visitors to see.

For starters, there's the white marble staircase with a huge antechamber which dates back to the time when Belgium was part of the Netherlands. There are paintings here of Leopold, the 1st King of Belgium, and his wife Princess Charlotte of Wales. She died a year after they married, due to complications following the birth of a stillborn baby. Interesting to think that had she lived she would have been Queen of England after the death of her father, King George IV. Instead, he was succeeded by his younger brother, William IV.

Rooms on the visitor route include the magnificent Empire Room, originally the ballroom, which contains the work 'Flowers of the Royal Palace' – eleven pots of earth and flowers from each of the country's provinces and the city of Brussels. The room is still used today for some ceremonial occasions. The Coburg Room is dedicated to paintings of the Saxe-Coburg family while the elegant Goya Room is where to see the three Spanish tapestries given to Leopold I by Queen Isabelle II of Spain, based on a drawing by Francisco Goya. The impressive Throne Room, with its parquet floor of oak and rare woods, was created by Leopold II and features reliefs by Rodin. One of the most unusual rooms is the Mirror Room, with its marble and copper walls. In 2002 artist Jan Fabre decorated the ceiling and a chandelier with over 1,500,000 jewel scarab wings. The effect is known as 'Heaven of Delight'.

Other notable rooms include the Thinker's Room, named after Michelangelo's famous statue, a miniature of which can be seen there, while the Pilaster Room houses a painting of Leopold I dating back to the 1840s.

Interesting facts about the Royal Palace:

• King Philippe's military career saw him qualify as a fighter pilot, parachutist and commando and he rose to the rank of major general in the army and rear admiral in the navy.

• If a flag is flying at the palace it means the king is in the country. If there is a royal guard it means he is in the palace.

• King Leopold II, an unfaithful husband who had an outrageous private life, was described by his cousin Queen Victoria as 'unfit and idle'.

Address: Royal Palace, Rue Brederode, 16, 1000 Brussels

Website:
www.monarchie.be/en/heritage/royal-palace-of-brussels

Visitor information: Open every day except Mondays during the season, which is around late July to early September. There is no admission charge. Despite its short opening time the palace welcomes over 100,000 visitors each year.

– CHANNEL ISLANDS –

CASTLE CORNET, GUERNSEY

Built on a rocky promontory in the sea, Castle Cornet has stood guard over St Peter Port harbour for the last 800 years. The name 'Cornet' is thought to have come from a family of merchants who lived on Guernsey at the time the castle was built.

In its early years the castle was the subject of a tug of war between local forces and the French. In fact, not just one tug of war, it was fought over time and time again between the 13th and 16th centuries. Every time, local forces managed to boot out the invaders but it was often touch and go. An attack in 1294 saw as much as a quarter of St Peter Port's population killed.

In the Middle Ages the structure consisted of a keep, a chapel, two courtyards and curtain walls. Between 1545 and 1548 the castle was modified to take into account the invention of gunpowder and thus cannon

Further down the line, a local civil war broke out mirroring the English Civil War. Governor Peter Osborne remained loyal to the King but the islanders were on the side of the Parliamentarians and besieged the castle. The castle retaliated by firing on the town of St Peter Port, reducing much of it to rubble. The governor and a small group of men were held in the castle receiving supplies by boat though eventually Osborne surrendered.

Twenty years later in 1672 the castle suffered a major catastrophe when the gunpowder-packed magazine housed in the donjon was struck by lightning in a December storm. The governor, Sir Christopher Hatton, was in bed but the force threw him onto the floor. He lived, but the explosion and falling rubble killed his wife, her maidservant and Hatton's mother, though the two children survived. The Governor's two sisters, a prisoner and some soldiers also lived to tell the tale.

After the Second World War, during which the castle had been occupied by German troops, it was presented by King George VI to the islanders in commemoration of the part they played in both world wars.

Four original gardens within the castle walls include the Governor's Garden planted in formal 17th-century style, and the kitchen garden for growing herbs, vegetables and fruit. Nearby, the 'plaisance', a relaxing area planted with roses and other decorative plants, has a camomile lawn. Resident officers like to spend their free time there. Lambert's Garden is close by the building where General Sir John Lambert was imprisoned in 1660 for his part in the English Civil War. It is planted with many of the same herbs and flowers he used to make medicinal remedies to treat the soldiers' ailments within the castle. The Master Gunner's Garden is set out in more modern 19th-century style but is east facing and therefore subject to salt-water air. It's tough to grow plants here and it is suggested it may have been used originally to keep domestic animals.

Interesting facts about Castle Cornet:

• The Maritime Museum in the castle is, as the name suggests, all about seafaring. A display is dedicated to Admiral James Saumarez, one of Guernsey's naval heroes.

Photo: Man vyi

• At noon every day a gun is fired by soldiers in 19th-century uniform. The tradition of firing a gun at noon dates from at least the beginning of the 19th century. The practice ceased in 1923 but was reintroduced in 1974. The soldiers are usually happy to pose for pictures with visitors.

• The Royal Guernsey Militia and related Royal Guernsey Light Infantry Museums are located in the castle's hospital building. The Royal Guernsey Militia Museum tells the story of the militia from its 13th-century origins as an island defence force to its 20th-century disbandment on the formation of the Royal Guernsey Light Infantry. The Royal Guernsey Light Infantry Museum tells the story of the Guernsey men who fought in the Great War.

Address: Castle Cornet, St Peter Port, Guernsey, GY1 6JN

Website: www.museums.gov.gg/article/101089/Castle-Cornet

Visitor information: The castle is a busy visitor attraction. It is initially open to the public from mid-February until late March but during this time there is no formal guided tour and the midday canon is not fired. These events start from late March and continue until early November. During this period the castle refectory is also open, offering visitors refreshments.

Most days during the visitor season, following the firing of the gun, the Guernsey History in Action Company re-enacts stories from Guernsey's past. The formal guided tour starts at 10.30am and there are also self-guided walks and a treasure hunt for children.

– CZECH REPUBLIC –

PRAGUE CASTLE, PRAGUE

The showstopper Prague Castle is actually one of a group of buildings. These include a medieval coronation hall, the world's largest toy museum, courtyards and the Gothic St Vitus Cathedral where Czech kings and queens were crowned.

Prague Castle towers above the old town. According to the Guinness Book of World Records, the site is the largest ancient castle complex in the world at 753,475 square feet. It looks like something straight from a fairy tale when darkness falls and it is illuminated by twinkling lights.

Archaeological research and old written sources suggest that the earliest building, made of wood, originated in 880. Since the 9th century, when Prince Bořivoj established a fortification here, the castle has been the seat of monarchs and official residence of the head of state.

Over the centuries the building was improved, rebuilt and fortifications strengthened. In 1485, King Ladislaus II Jagiello added the enormous Vladislav Hall together with new defence towers on the north side of the castle. Then in 1526 the Habsburg dynasty took over the Czech throne and the seat of power moved to Vienna. This left Prague Castle to be used mainly for recreational purposes until a fire in 1541 destroyed most of it. However, under Habsburg orders, over the following years several Renaissance style buildings were added. The reconstruction culminated during the reign of Holy Roman Emperor Rudolf II who, when he became Czech king in 1575, moved his court back to Prague.

The Second Defenestration of Prague in 1618 took place at the castle and began the Bohemian Revolt, often called the Thirty Years' War. The word 'defenestration' means throwing someone out of a window and that is exactly what happened here. Catholic officials decided to close a Protestant church and this annoyed a number of Protestants, who called for a trial at the castle. They won. This meant that two Catholic regents and their secretary, found guilty of violating the right to religious freedom, were unceremoniously thrown out of the window. Luck must have been on their side though because they landed in a pile of horse manure and walked away uninjured. Over the years there have been other less noteworthy defenestrations in Prague.

As might be expected, the castle experienced damage during subsequent wars. The last major rebuilding of the castle was carried out by Empress Maria Theresa, a fierce but fair ruler, in the second half of the 18th century.

Following his abdication in 1848 and the succession of his nephew Franz Joseph to the throne, former Emperor Ferdinand I made Prague Castle his home. Then in 1918, the castle became the seat of the President of the new Czechoslovak Republic, T.G. Masaryk. On 15 March 1939, shortly after Nazi Germany forced Czech President Emil Hacha – who suffered a heart attack during the negotiations – to hand his nation over to the Germans, Adolf Hitler spent a night in Prague Castle, it was said, 'proudly surveying his new possession'.

During the Nazi occupation of Czechoslovakia in the Second World War, Prague Castle became the headquarters of Reinhard Heydrich, the Reich Protector of Bohemia and Moravia. According to stories, he fancied his own importance and placed the Bohemian crown on his own head. He should have taken heed of legend, which says a usurper who wears the crown will die within a year. Yes, exactly. On 27 May 1942, less than a year after assuming power, Heydrich was attacked during Operation Anthropoid by British-trained Slovak and Czech soldiers while on his way to the Castle. He died the following week of his wounds which became infected. Klaus, his firstborn son, died the next year in a traffic accident, also in line with the legend.

After the liberation of Czechoslovakia and the coup in 1948, the castle housed the offices of the communist Czechoslovak government. Then after the country was split into the Czech Republic and Slovakia, the castle became the seat of the Head of State of the new Czech Republic.

After the fall of communism in 1989, many of the castle's previously off-limit areas were reopened to the public. Now visitors can see the Imperial Stables and exhibition halls and wander round some of the creaky-floored rooms. They can also enjoy a stroll through the Royal Garden. The South Gardens include Archduke Ferdinand's 16th-century Paradise Garden with a 400-year-old yew tree, one of the castle's oldest trees.

Interesting facts about Prague Castle:

• The castle was the seat of power for kings of Bohemia, Holy Roman emperors and presidents of Czechoslovakia.

• The interior of St Vitus Cathedral at the heart of the castle features stained glass, royal tombs and relics of the country's patron saints. The Bohemian Crown Jewels are kept here too. For safekeeping the chamber door and iron safe inside have seven locks, the keys to which are held by

Photo: Tilman2007

seven people, including the President and Prime Minister. Since 1997 St Vitus Cathedral's full name is the Cathedral of Sts Vita, Václava and Vojtěcha. So there you have it.

• Behind the castle is a street called Golden Lane where in the 16th century, alchemists under Emperor Rudolph III lived. They spent their time attempting to turn metal into gold, well so the story goes. It is more likely that goldsmiths lived here and it was they who gave the street its name.

Address: Prague Castle, 119 08 Prague

Website: www.hrad.cz/en/prague-castle-for-visitors

Visitor information: Prague Castle is one of the most visited tourist attractions in Prague, attracting over 1.8 million visitors annually. Most areas of the castle are open to tourists.

The castle houses several museums including the National Gallery collection of Bohemian baroque and mannerism art, an exhibition dedicated to Czech history, the Toy Museum and a picture gallery based on the collection of Rudolph II.

– DENMARK –

KRONBORG CASTLE, HELSINGØR

A fortified castle in the Danish town of Helsingør, Kronborg Castle was the setting for Shakespeare's play Hamlet, *where it was known as Elsinor. It became a UNESCO World Heritage Site in 2000.*

The castle lords over the northernmost point of Zealand on the Øresund (the Sound) which separates Denmark and Sweden, though at the time the castle was constructed the area that is now Sweden belonged to Denmark.

It was built in the 1420s by King Eric of Pomerania as one of a pair that stood either side of the Øresund, standing guard over the entrance to the Baltic Sea. Because of its position, Kronborg generated significant revenues by collecting tolls from ships using the Sound.

In the late 16th century the then king, Frederick, a keen supporter of the arts, carried out extensive reconstruction on the original medieval structure to create a look-at-me Renaissance castle. It was after this that the castle acquired its current name of Kronborg, which translated into English means 'Crown Castle'. It was around that time too that the castle became a venue for theatrical performances and an English acting troupe performed in Helsingør. Some of the actors are said to have later worked with Shakespeare, no doubt giving the playwright eyewitness accounts of Kronborg's assets.

The newly done up castle included three wings, one of which provided accommodation for the king, queen and her ladies in waiting. The other two housed a chapel and a ballroom respectively. Originally just two storeys high, a third level was added to include a magnificent marble-floored ballroom, a 'must-have' in those days. It measured 62 by 12 metres (200 by 40 feet) and is where the king's servants hung tapestries on the walls for special occasions. At such times the king would hold court at one end of the room next to a large fireplace.

In 1629 the castle suffered severe damage when fire tore through it, with only the chapel surviving. A year later, under King Christian IV, rebuilding work began and over

Photo: Dennis Jarvis

the following ten years the castle's exterior was restored to its former glory. The interior however was rebuilt to include several baroque features that were not in the earlier structure.

During two years of war between Denmark and Sweden in 1658–60, the castle was held under siege and plundered of its treasures. Clearly there were serious flaws in the castle's defences and following the siege these were improved to include ramparts. That made it significantly more secure.

Then no longer a royal palace, the castle was used as a military barracks and prison from 1739 to the 1900s. Prisoners were set to work in chain gangs to repair and improve the castle's defences. Minor offenders were classed as 'honest' and were allowed to work outside the castle confines. Serious offenders, murderers and the like, were classed as 'dishonest' and were sentenced to hard labour inside the castle ramparts. Both classes of offenders had to wear chains and spend nights in horrid cold, damp dungeons.

In 1923 the army left the barracks and restoration began on the castle, which is now a major Danish tourist attraction, hosting over a quarter of a million visitors a year.

Of course, the link with Shakespeare and his play *The Tragedy of Hamlet, Prince of Denmark* is one of the castle's best-known claims to fame. However, Shakespeare never visited Denmark, let alone Kronborg Castle and there was no Prince of Denmark called Hamlet. It is believed he may have got this name from stories about Amled, a prince from Jutland. Nevertheless, each summer a number of theatrical companies, including the Royal Shakespeare Company, put on public performances of Shakespeare's play in the open air, at the venue. Afterwards, visitors can stand on the sites where key elements of the story took place.

Today the castle has many attractions for visitors, not just the link to Shakespeare and his famous play. The royal apartments in the north wing on the first floor are furnished with 17th-century locally-made items. Many of the ballroom's fittings were lost to fire and looting but the remainder give visitors an idea of what it would have been like in its heyday. The ballroom offers seating for up to 420 people for functions and celebrations.

A marble and alabaster altar is the showpiece of the chapel, which is on the ground floor of the south wing. It dates back to 1582, having survived the fire mentioned earlier. When it was being converted to an army barracks in the late 18th century, furnishings were removed and the chapel was used for fencing and other physical activities. In the mid-19th century the original furniture was put back and the chapel restored with colourful carved pews. Today it serves as a parish church and is a popular wedding venue.

The kings of Denmark and Sweden were constantly trying to out-do each other. When King Erik XIV of Sweden commissioned tapestries depicting his family's history, the Danish King Frederick II went one better and commissioned 43 tapestries depicting a thousand years of kings and princes. Today there are only fifteen surviving tapestries, of which seven are at the castle.

Interesting facts about Kronborg Castle:

• King Eric of Pomerania must have been quite a catch by all accounts, or at least by the account of (the future) Pope, Pius II, who described the King as having 'a beautiful body, reddish yellow hair, a ruddy face, and a long narrow neck and all women were drawn to him…' Interestingly, when king Eric was dethroned in 1439 for causing all sorts of problems, he fled from his kingship duties to become leader of a group of pirates who terrorised merchant vessels on the Baltic Sea.

• Many famous actors have taken part in performances of *Hamlet* at the castle. They include Sir Laurence Olivier, Vivien Leigh, Sir John Gielgud, Richard Burton, Christopher Plummer, Derek Jacobi, Kenneth Branagh, Simon Russell Beale and Jude Law.

• Visitors to the castle dungeons will see the statue of a sleeping Holger the Dane. The story has it that if ever Denmark is in trouble, Holger will wake up and save the country.

Address: Kronborg Castle, Kronborg 2 C, 3000 Helsingør

Website:
http://kongeligeslotte.dk/en/palaces-and-gardens/
kronborg-castle.html

Visitor Information: The castle, which is open year-round for visitors, is also used as a venue for events including dinners, conferences and wedding receptions, which may follow a ceremony in the castle's chapel. Guests can be greeted with a trumpet fanfare from the high tower as they enter the castle – how's that for a welcome with a difference?

– FRANCE –

CHÂTEAU DE FONTAINEBLEAU, FONTAINEBLEAU

The Château de Fontainebleau is one of the oldest and largest castles in France. It is located 34 miles (55 kilometres) from Paris. Records show that a fortified structure existed on the site as early as 1137. After that the château was a residence for French monarchs from Francois I to Napoleon III.

Used by the kings of France from the 12th century, the hunting lodge of Fontainebleau, standing in the heart of the vast forest of the Île-de-France in the Seine-et-Marne region, was enlarged and embellished in the 16th century by King François I.

Fontainebleau is the only royal château to have been continuously inhabited for seven centuries. Thirty-four kings and two emperors lived here. In fact anybody who was anybody stayed here – kings, queens, emperors, empresses, dukes, duchesses – and this is where they liked to entertain the big names of the day. In Louis XIV's time Queen Christina of Sweden came to stay just after she had given up her crown. While she was at Fontainebleau she got annoyed because she was told that her lover, who was with her, had divulged certain secrets to her enemies. She wasn't going to stand for that and got her servants to finish him off. Whether her host, Louis, knew about it or not – you'd think he would have – it wasn't mentioned between them. She continued on her travels after leaving Fontainebleau.

Russian Tsar Peter the Great also came to visit, though he was somewhat unenthusiastic about his stay – the castle was smaller than he would have liked and he preferred to drink beer rather than wine.

But the kings and queens, emperors and empresses who lived at Fontainebleau all liked it enough to want to make improvements to it. King Henry IV (known as Good King Henry) went to town and even added an indoor tennis court – the largest in the world at the time. Louis XV built a new courtyard and Louis XVI added a games room for Marie Antoinette – apparently she once spent three days in there gambling non-stop. Napoleon Bonaparte also adored Fontainebleau and he did quite a bit of work on it too, refurnishing and redecorating.

In September 1725 the castle was the scene of a grand wedding when fifteen-year-old Louis XV married 22-year-old Polish Princess Marie. Their first meeting was on the eve of their wedding. Diarists of the time reported that the new Queen, done up to the nines, almost passed out under the weight of her jewel-encrusted finery.

Today the interior is as breathtakingly magnificent as ever and although visitors can't see in all of the 1,500 or so rooms, they can gasp in awe at those that they do. Things to see include the emperor Napoleon's famous hats, his gold-embroidered ceremonial suits and the silver travelling set which he took everywhere with him. There is his sword too, his Sèvres porcelain services and portraits of the man himself. The table displayed in his small salon is where he signed his abdication in 1814.

The 16th-century ballroom with windows overlooking the oval courtyard and gardens is famed for its mythological frescoes, marquetry floor and Italian-inspired ceiling. The longest room is the gallery of Diana, named after the goddess of hunting, created in the 17th century by Henry IV and turned into a library by Napoleon III.

The original bedroom of the kings was transformed into a throne room by Napoleon in 1808 while the Papal Apartment was so named following two visits by Pope Pius VII in 1808 and 1812. Most carved wood panels adorning the ceiling date back to Louis XIII's day, although the ceiling over the throne is attributed to the time of Louis XV. The interesting Chinese Museum was built for Empress Eugenie in 1863 for her collection of Far Eastern treasures. Some of these were brought from the Summer Palace in Beijing as soldiers' plunder, while others were gifts from the King of Siam.

When you've visited the interior, leave enough time to visit the gardens. The Grand Parterre is said to be Europe's largest formal garden while the smaller English Garden has an artificial river. The Diana Garden has as its focal point a fountain with a statue of the goddess herself.

Just before the First World War the building was declared a historical monument and officially became a museum in 1927. It was occupied by the Germans during the Second World War but later became the NATO headquarters of the Allied Forces in Central Europe. President Charles de Gaulle was responsible for the restoration of the château in the mid 1960s and it was later designated a UNESCO World Heritage Site.

Interesting facts about the Château de Fontainebleau:

• 'The true residence of kings' was how Napoleon described the castle in August 1816.

• The name Fontainebleau comes from one of the many springs in the area, the fountain de Bliaud, which is now in the English Garden.

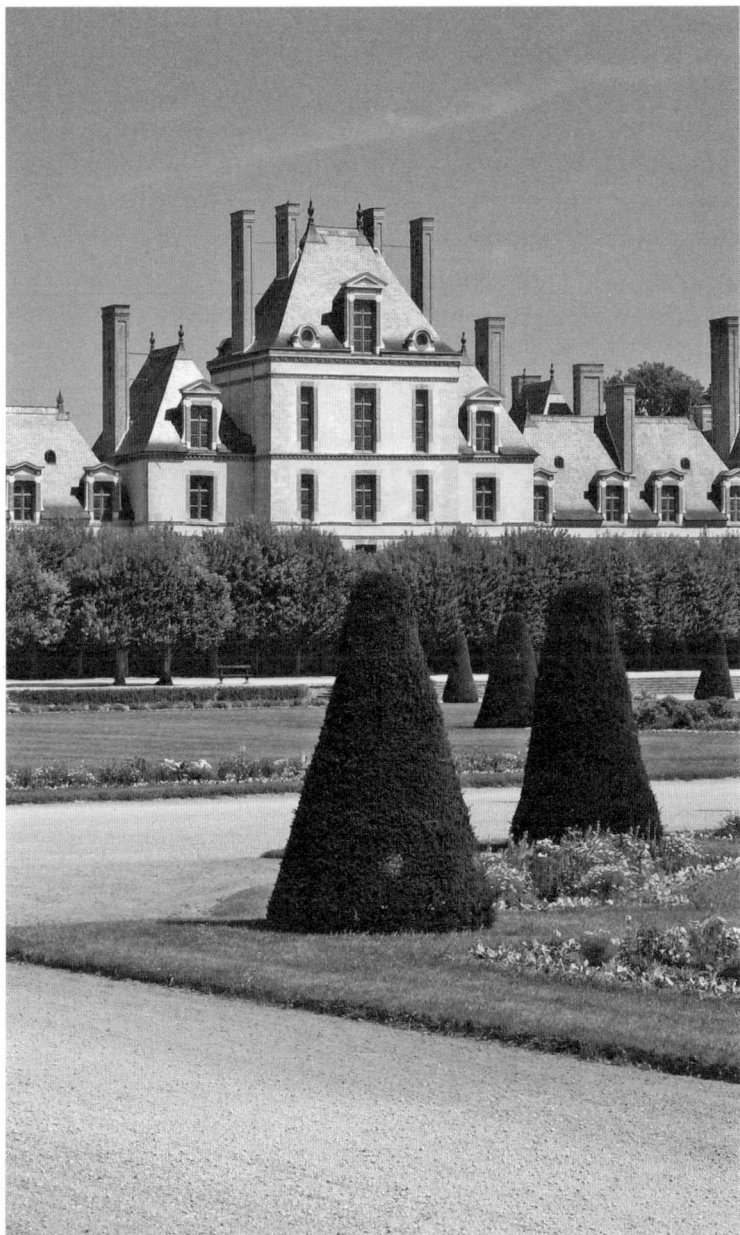

Photo: Basvb

• Seventeenth-century writings tell of guests feeding the carp in the pond, some of which reached enormous size and were said to be over 100 years old. Probably an exaggeration.

Address: Château de Fontainebleau, 77300 Fontainebleau

Website: www.chateaudefontainebleau.fr

Visitor information: The castle is open every day except Tuesdays, while the courtyards and garden are open daily. There is a lift to transport those with limited mobility to the grand apartments. Visitors to the gardens can enjoy a game of real tennis, Segway rides, boating or a hot-air balloon trip. Those who prefer not to walk round the gardens can hop on the train for the 30–45 minute trip. Audio guides in seven languages are available.

CHÂTEAU DE PIERREFONDS, PICARDY

A blend of flamboyant Gothic and romantic Renaissance styles, the castle which lies on the edge of the Forest of Compiègne dominates the pretty village of Pierrefonds, 60 miles north-east of Paris.

Plucked straight from a fairy tale, the imposing Château de Pierrefonds has the lot – from crenellated towers, a drawbridge and moat to an array of multi-level turrets. It oozes romance.

In the 12th century a castle was built on the site as part of the County of Valois. When the House of Valois ascended the throne of France in 1328, Pierrefonds passed into the royal domain. The original castle was replaced by this showstopper, which was constructed in the 14th century by Louis I, Duke of Orléans. He converted the site into one of France's largest fortresses. Work was just coming to an end when the Duke's assassination in 1407 brought an immediate cessation to building work. Pierrefonds Castle then suffered a severe storming by Cardinal Richelieu's troops in 1617. They thought it would be a great idea to dismantle the castle and it remained in this sad state of ruin for the next couple of hundred years.

In 1810 Napoleon I happened along. He was looking around for something to buy and acquired it at a ridiculously low price. He didn't really do anything with it and a few years further down the line in 1848 it was classified as a national heritage building by the French Ministry of Culture.

Some years later the ruins were visited by the showy Louis-Napoleon Bonaparte, who later became Napoleon III. He was nephew of the aforesaid Napoleon I. By this time, things had changed quite a bit and the village of Pierrefonds had become popular with wealthy visitors, drawn by its thermal waters. The ruins, once regarded as ugly, were now seen as charming and served as a backdrop and inspiration for artists, painters and poets.

In 1857, although at that time he had no intention of living there, Napoleon III decided he would commission leading French architect of the day, Eugène Viollet-le-Duc, to apply his architectural designs to create the ideal château, such as would have existed in the Middle Ages. Parts were left as picturesque ruins, the rest was rebuilt and a riot of gargoyles, arches and galleries were added. However, some years later Napoleon III changed his mind and decided to go the whole hog and make Pierrefonds one of his residences. Trusty Viollet-le-Duc was brought back into service to restore the castle completely.

Photo: P.poschadel

Although Napoleon III died in 1873 and Viollet-le-Duc in 1879, the renovation works did not stop until 1885. However, decoration of the rooms remained unfinished due to lack of funds. Nevertheless to this day, it remains Viollet-le-Duc's crowning achievement, a masterpiece of pomp and circumstance. He certainly lived up to the motto of the lords of Pierrefonds: 'He who wants to, can!'

What would a photogenic fairy-tale castle be without a dungeon or two? Pierrefonds, *oubliettes* – underground dungeons – were of the type commonly found in medieval castles. A single trap door at the top was the only entrance to the dungeon, which was accessible via a rope or a ladder. Besides dungeons, the castle comes with moat, drawbridge, arrow slits and seven-metre-thick battlemented walls surrounding a courtyard.

It is no wonder Pierrefonds has been a mainstay in television and movies and has been the location for many swashbuckling French films, including *The Messenger: The Story of Joan of Arc* (1999). You might have seen it in the 1998 Leonardo DiCaprio film, *The Man in the Iron Mask* too. Besides that, it made an appearance in the Disney television show 'Wizards of Waverly Place' (2007–12) and what's more, its fame spread to the UK when it stood in for Camelot in the BBC series 'Merlin' (2008–12). Think how delighted Viollet-le-Duc would have been ….

If you can arrange a visit, do go. It is well worth it. You can spend ages meandering round its 132 magnificent rooms, climbing its 5,445 steps and admiring the 100-odd fireplaces – some are exceptionally glorious (and huge). If you ask the guide nicely, she might even let you inside the Echo Chamber – it's fun.

Besides all that, you will enjoy the feeling of being in a jolly important place with a wonderful history.

Interesting facts about Pierrefonds Castle:

• The timber-ceilinged hall in the Salle des Preuses is shaped like an upturned ship.

• Each of the eight soaring towers is dedicated to a different knight.

• In 1832 King Louis-Philippe held a banquet in Pierrefonds Castle on the occasion of his daughter's marriage to Leopold of Saxe-Coburg-Gotha, 1st King of Belgium.

Address: Château de Pierrefonds, Rue Viollet le Duc, 60350 Pierrefonds, Picardy

Websites: www.chateau-pierrefonds.fr
www.pierrefonds.monuments-nationaux.fr

Visitor information: Pierrefonds makes a great day out for the whole family. Kids of all ages love the parapet walk, imperial apartments with period decor and the family activities which take place regularly.

PALACE OF VERSAILLES, VERSAILLES

One of the world's most famous palaces, and inspiration for St Petersburg's Peterhof Palace, Versailles hosts 5 million visitors a year.

Originally a small village in the midst of extensive woodlands, Versailles was an area visited by King Henry IV's son Louis on his first hunting trip in 1602. On the death of his father he became King Louis XIII and returned to the area a few years later to build a hunting lodge. A modest structure, even by the standards of the time, he expanded it and thereafter his son, who would become Louis XIV, the 'Sun King' – he took the sun as his emblem – first visited as a boy and returned as king years later. Yes, the name Louis was popular at the time and Louis XIV was determined to ensure that the next King of France was going to be called Louis too. Heirs to the throne – Louis XIV's eldest son, grandson, great-grandson and great-grandson's brother – were all called Louis, so future kings were Louis XV, Louis XVI, Louis XVII and Louis XVIII.

When Louis XIV expanded the opulent pile that was Versailles in the late 1600s, it became the envy of many other European monarchs. The royal court and seat of government were established there in 1682 when Louis moved the royal court from the Louvre, Paris. Until his death in 1715 he embarked on construction work to expand and upgrade the palace and gardens. He also spent time dallying with the ladies and his wife Maria Theresa, a Spanish princess, often felt lonely. She didn't speak French very well and surrounded herself with Spanish ladies-in-waiting. Louise de La Vallière was one of Louis' mistresses and bore several of his children. He and Maria Theresa were married only three years before she died and Louis remarried two years later. His second wife, Françoise d'Aubigné, Marquise de Maintenon, was of a lower social standing so the marriage was kept as secret as it could be. However, it was something of an open secret. Incidentally, the American state of Louisiana is named after Louis XIV. It was under French control between 1682 and 1763 and again from 1800–3, and was known as La Louisiane (Land of Louis).

Following Louis XIV's death, Versailles was visited by Russian Tsar Peter the Great in 1717. He was well impressed and inspired by its opulence and thought it would be a good idea to create something along those lines for himself when he returned home. The result was the Peterhof Palace which is located near St Petersburg. (See page 194.)

Louis XV finished the work originally planned by his predecessors, which included the construction of the Royal Opera House, and this was where his son married Archduchess Marie Antoinette. Having contracted smallpox, Louis XV returned to the palace, where he died in 1774.

Versailles remained the royal family home until the royals had to return to Paris in 1789, around three months after the French Revolution started and peasants stormed the castle. Despite its association with the then despised royalty, the palace didn't get damaged too much and when the monarchy was no more, maintenance became the responsibility of government. Works of art were removed and furniture sold off, but the palace remained a visitor attraction. Versailles is therefore famous not only as a building, but as a symbol of the system of absolute monarchy of the Ancien Régime.

The palace became the Museum of the History of France and opened in 1837. The collection of paintings and sculptures grew over the years and Versailles regained much of its earlier importance. Napoleon III played host there to Queen Victoria in 1855.

The palace emerged largely undamaged from the First World War but lack of post-war funds meant that little maintenance was carried out. American billionaire John D. Rockefeller made substantial donations to allow restoration to proceed. Years later the French government recognised its importance and hosted official visits from world dignitaries including HM Queen Elizabeth II and the

Photo: ToucanWings

Kennedys. The 1982 G7 summit was also held at Versailles.

Visitors can see the grand Hall of Mirrors where magnificent balls were held, as well as state apartments, private apartments and Marie Antoinette's bedroom, while the elaborately fashioned grounds, brimful of fountains, gardens and mazes, are a visitor attraction in their own right.

Interesting facts about the Palace of Versailles:

• Versailles has a whopping 2,300 rooms, 67 staircases and 5,210 pieces of furniture spread over 75,000 square yards and there is a mile-long canal within the 2,000-acre gardens. And since there's a lot of numbers here, I'll also say there are 2,400 fountains and 230 acres of ornamental terraces in the grounds.

• The Palace of Versailles was the location of the first hot-air balloon flight or 'aerostatic' flight as it was called then, in 1783.

• Louis XIV owned over 1,000 wigs and 413 beds. Pictures show him dressed in high heels with big hair, the reason being it made him look taller. He was only five-foot-four-inches tall and in heels and a wig he would appear almost seven feet tall. Incidentally, some history books tell that he was born with two teeth, though I cannot say for sure whether or not this is true.

Address: Palace of Versailles, Place d'Armes, 78000 Versailles

Website: http://en.chateauversailles.fr/

Visitor information: The palace is open every day except Mondays. The gardens and park are open every day. Access to the gardens is free except on days when there is a Musical Fountains Show. Guided tours allow visitors to view otherwise closed rooms. Don't miss the Hameau de la Reine, a rustic cottage in the grounds where Marie-Antoinette would go to escape hectic court life and pretend to be a shepherdess.

For those looking for an alternative to exploring on foot there is bicycle hire, a visitor train, electric buggies, Segways and rowing boats on the lake.

– GERMANY –

NEUSCHWANSTEIN CASTLE, SCHWANGAU

Among Bavaria's medieval villages, flowery meadows and dark forests is the straight–from-a-fairy-tale Schloss Neuschwanstein, a 19th-century Romanesque Revival fantasy castle which belonged to that delightfully eccentric monarch, Ludwig II.

This cracking palace, which stands 3,000 feet above sea level, has king-of-the-world views. It was part of the inspiration behind Tchaikovsky's *Swan Lake* and I wonder what His Majesty would have thought if he knew it was used as the model for Disney's *Cinderella* palace?

The name Neuschwanstein literally means 'New Swan Stone' which comes from one of Wagner's operas, *The Swan Knight (Lohengrin)*. Ludwig adored swans and the swan motif is repeated many times throughout the castle interior on fabrics and as wood carvings; even the water taps are elegantly shaped like swans. The swan represents

Photo: Rachel Davis

not only purity but also the character of the Swan Knight in *Lohengrin*. The composer was much admired by the highly artistic Ludwig, who was also a great friend. As a recluse, Ludwig identified with the Swan Knight to such an extent that he sometimes dressed as him.

While hundreds of craftsmen toiled to produce his dream castle, Ludwig would spend hours with his telescope watching progress from the mountain opposite. During construction he wrote to Wagner, 'The location is one of the most beautiful to be found, holy and unapproachable, a worthy temple …'

Theatrical designers and artisans worked alongside architects in the creation of his dream and it took 50 of them two years to carve only his bed. Neuschwanstein was built at a time when castles didn't have to be strongholds and Ludwig decided it should have all the latest technological comforts. The lavish structure had running water throughout, flush toilets, hot water in the kitchen and bathrooms as well as a forced-air central heating system.

He ordered a pulley system to be installed which enabled the dining table to be lowered from the dining room to the kitchen because he preferred not to see the servants more than necessary. Sometimes his manners were less than exemplary and he would spill food on the table, spit at his servants and pour drinks over them. He introduced Chinese court etiquette which meant footmen had to bow right down to their feet when they saw him. He was the most reclusive of kings and hardly ever had real visitors, preferring to invite imaginary guests to dinner.

One visitor he did enjoy entertaining was Wagner. When Wagner stayed, Ludwig arranged for his morning call to be delivered by oboists standing on top of the castle towers, playing snatches from the composer's operas. He would also request private performances of Wagner's operas because he didn't want anyone staring at him during a public performance.

At times he would order his table to be set for up to four people, so that Louis XIV or Madame Pompadour could join him in spirit. On a couple of occasions, he even ate dinner with his horse positioned at the other end of the banquet table. If he did have visitors to dine, he would hide behind masses of flowers and shrubbery which he would tell the servants to put in front of his dinner plate. On these occasions he also ordered music to be played exceptionally loudly so that conversation would be kept to a minimum.

In keeping with its romantic design, the castle's two-level throne room, which still did not contain a throne at the time of Ludwig's death, is modelled after a byzantine basilica with stars decorating its blue vaulted ceiling. He also had a mini-grotto constructed next to his study with artificial stalagmites and stalactites. The ballroom is decorated in the theme of *Parsifal*, another of Wagner's operas. Although at the time of the King's death the castle was unfinished, with only fourteen of the 200 rooms complete, he first occupied his residential quarters in May 1884. Visitors today can see these, as well as the servant's rooms, kitchens and Throne Room.

Ludwig was often referred to as the 'Fairy tale King' or the 'Mad King' although research suggests that he was highly eccentric rather than clinically insane. While living in Neuschwanstein, he increasingly went to bed in the morning and got up around 5pm, so perhaps it was no surprise that his eccentric ways and extravagance worried the Bavarian government. He had amassed debts of many millions of marks too. Eventually, at around midnight on 12 June 1886, psychiatrists were dispatched to his beloved castle to certify poor Ludwig insane, at the request of the government. Just before that he seemed to sense that his time was coming to an end and requested potassium cyanide from a doctor friend. He wrote: 'Hurtling downward from the highest levels of life into nothingness. That is a lost life and I cannot bear it.'

On 13 June 1886, both he and his doctor were found dead, drowned in Lake Starnberg – accident or assassination? To this day no one knows. Bavarians say that Ludwig was a strong swimmer, he would not have drowned. They are sure he was murdered.

Interesting facts about Neuschwanstein Castle and King Ludwig (because you can't really have one without the other):

• In Linderhof Palace, another of his grand castles, Ludwig continued the swan theme and there is a gold swan boat in the Venus Grotto which he liked to sit in and listen to operatic arias. He also owned the golden-yellow Schloss Hohenschwangau, the mock Tudor family seat built by his father, Crown Prince Maximilian, which lies in the shadow of Neuschwanstein and is still owned by the Wittelsbach family; one of the oldest German dynasties.

• In the environs of his other castles, Ludwig liked to go out on night rides on his sleigh, which was the first in the world to be electric-lit. Before electricity it had a battery under the driver's seat to power glass lamps at the front. Ludwig had his craftsmen design submarines and peacock carts that sailed through the air. He also instructed them to build him a hunting lodge with a great hall 1,866 metres high on a mountain. He liked to go there to smoke water pipes but did not go hunting.

- *Chitty Chitty Bang Bang* (1968) and *The Wonderful World of the Brothers Grimm* (1962) are two films in which Neuschwanstein Castle features.

Address: Neuschwanstein Castle, Schwangau, Bavaria

Website: www.neuschwanstein.de/englisch/tourist/index.htm

Visitor's information: This is one of Germany's biggest tourist attractions and its most photographed castle. More than 1.3 million people visit annually. Be prepared for lengthy queues when visiting at peak times in summer.

– HUNGARY –

BUDA CASTLE, BUDAPEST

The Siamese-twin city of Budapest, Hungary's capital, sits astride the river Danube which divides hilly Buda from flat Pest. This historical castle and palace complex which sits atop a hill is sometimes referred to as the Royal Palace, the ancient seat of royal power.

Buildings on both sides of the river are illuminated at night and an evening Danube cruise is a great way to admire structures including the riverside parliament building in Pest, inspired by London's Palace of Westminster, and Buda Castle which has had a chequered history.

Following the Mongolian invasion, the first palace was completed in 1265 on what became known as Castle Hill and was extended over the next couple of centuries to become Europe's largest Gothic palace.

In 1476 King Matthias Corvinus – Corvinus is derived from the Latin for 'raven' hence his 'Raven King' sobriquet – married Beatrix of Naples. Beatrix was obviously prettier than her sister Leonora because Matthias had already turned Leonora down due to her looks. Anyway, Beatrix brought with her craftsmen and artists working in the Renaissance style who set about transforming Buda and the palace. Soon it became the most famous court in Europe.

In 1526 the Turks of the Ottoman Empire happened along and destroyed Buda but the palace remained intact. Since then the royal palace has been destroyed and rebuilt several times including in 1686 when a large force of Christian military besieged the city and, in the process, destroyed most of the palace. The remaining parts were left to decay.

In 1715 another attempt was made to build a small baroque palace. Although it was later destroyed by fire, the core of the current palace was reconstructed on the same basis and is central to the current building. It forms part of the Budapest Historical Museum.

More rebuilding took place in the 1850s when Austrian Emperor Franz Joseph visited and it was here that he was crowned King of Hungary in 1857. Further down the line the government embarked on an ambitious development project in the area. They wanted it to compete with its more famous rival, Vienna, just along the river and in 1916 the palace took centre stage in the coronation of the last Hungarian king, Charles IV. Interestingly, the King's coronation ceremony on 30 December 1916 was recorded on film – the director of the documentary was Hungarian-born Michael Curtiz, who later won an Academy Award in 1942 for *Casablanca*.

The castle was briefly occupied by German military forces

during the Second World War, and then in 1945, following a siege by the Soviet Red Army, it was again destroyed by military action.

After the war, much research and excavation took place to determine what the castle, in its various forms, would have looked like had it not been destroyed multiple times. It was obviously difficult to come to a decision because it wasn't until 1958 that rebuilding work started. It was completed four years later.

Today the palace houses the Historical Museum of Budapest, which occupies four floors of the southern wing and gives an insight into the area's history and culture. It is a treasure chest of goodies with architectural findings that are more than 40,000 years old, posters from the 20th century, Gothic statues unearthed in 1974 and a 14th-century Anjou silk tapestry discovered in 1999. The Hungarian National Gallery, which has an overwhelming collection of paintings, sculptures and prints, is divided into six sections covering items from Gothic to contemporary work.

The National Library was founded in 1802 by Count Ferenc Széchényi, who travelled widely buying Hungarian books which he donated to the library. It was later opened to the public and now contains many written relics from Hungary's past. Incidentally, the youngest of Count Ferenc Széchényi's children, István Széchenyi, was responsible for the Chain Bridge that runs from the foot of Castle Hill in Buda across the Danube to Pest. For centuries, Buda and Pest were linked only by a pontoon bridge. In 1820 István Széchényi heard that his father had died in Vienna, and he was subsequently buried in Pest. The pontoon bridge was regularly unusable in winter weather so István, in Buda, found difficulty in visiting his father's grave. He decided to build a permanent river crossing, only the second such

Photo: Alex Proimos

crossing of the river Danube at that time. In 1836 he commissioned English engineer William Tierney Clark to design a bridge. In 1842 construction started, supervised by Scottish engineer Adam Clark, no relation to William. It was completed seven years later. During the Red Army's siege of Budapest in 1945 the Germans blew up the bridge. It was rebuilt in its original form and reopened after the war in 1949, and today forms an important link between Buda and Pest, especially the royal palace and is, for most visitors, the most popular way to approach the palace.

Interesting facts about Buda Castle:

• The House of Houdini is a museum and performance venue within the walls of Buda Castle. It presents the life of the Hungarian-born illusionist, Harry Houdini. Visitors can marvel at the magician's exhibits or take in a show while there. Check the website for opening hours.

• The Hospital in the Rock Nuclear Bunker Museum can be visited in the caverns under Buda Castle. The hospital was set up in the 1930s in preparation for the Second World War. Today the beds in one ward hold lifelike wax figures of soldiers depicting scenes from when it was first in use.

• A series of caves under Buda Castle once held prisoner Vlad Tepes or Vlad the Impaler, better known as Count Dracula, as legend has it.

Address: Buda Castle, Szent György tér 2, Budapest 1014

Website: http://budacastlebudapest.com

Visitor information: Reach Buda Castle by cable car (Sikló) from Adam Clark square at the Buda end of the Chain Bridge. It stops right in front of the castle and the journey takes less than ten minutes. Those who feel energetic can walk up the zig-zag pathway from the foot of the hill or hop on the castle bus which runs every few minutes from Moszkva Square.

– ITALY –

DOGE'S PALACE, VENICE

For centuries the Doge's Palace was the residence of the Doge, the ruler of Venice and seat of power for the Venetian Republic.

The Doge's Palace or Palazzo Ducale is one of the highlights for visitors to the Italian city, an island republic which was one of the powerhouses of European politics between the 12th and 16th centuries. Of all the wonderful locations for palaces, this palace must have one of the best.

In 810 a wooden palace was built on this site though later ravaged by fire. A few centuries later, when Venice began to grow as an important trading centre, a new palace was built to show off the city's burgeoning wealth and importance. Designs for the palace were created by Filippo Calendario, an architect who was later executed for treason. Work on the building, a pleasing mix of Byzantine and Gothic styles peppered with pink Verona marble and white Istrian stone, began around 1340. Besides the doge's private apartments,

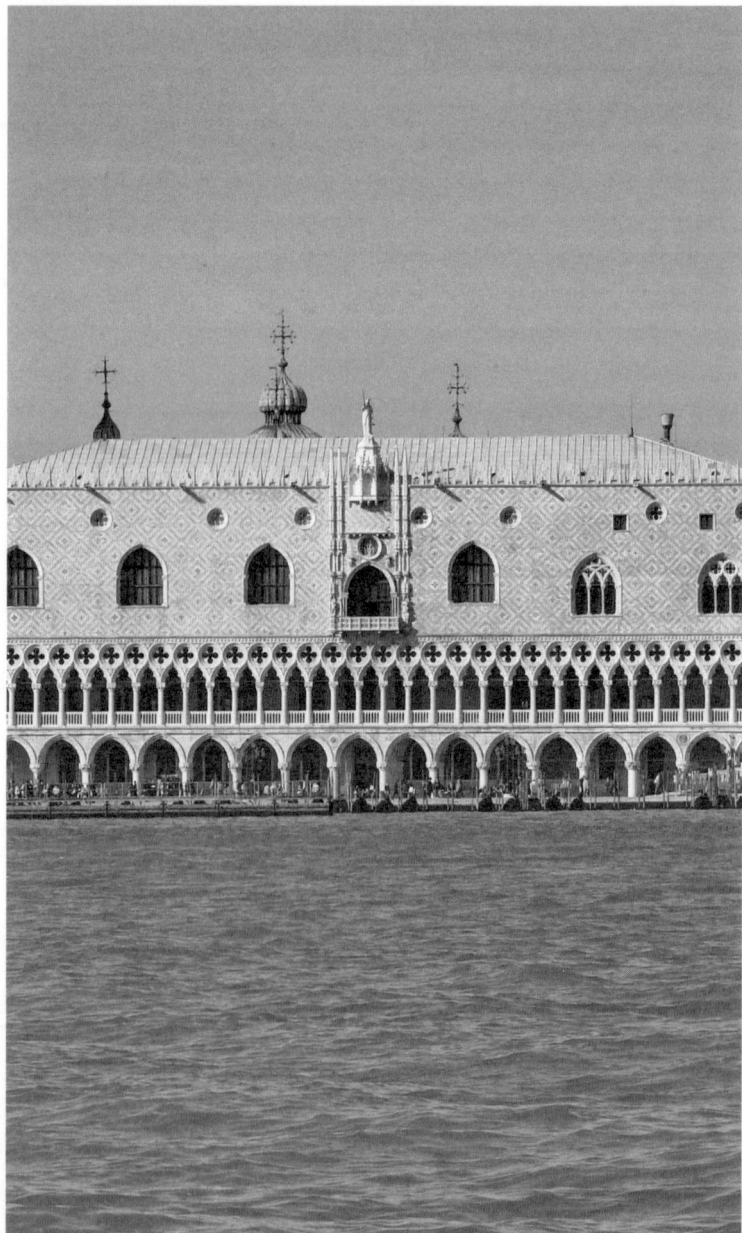

Photo: Inselmann

this lavish complex contained institutional offices and judicial chambers where financial affairs were discussed and sentences handed out by the criminal courts. It had courtyards, grand stairways, ballrooms and prisons too, all of which can still be seen today.

Its cells were usually busy, with some prisoners being kept in more uncomfortable surroundings than others. There was a block called the Piombi, which was underneath the lead roof. These cells became as hot as ovens in summer while in the depths of winter were seriously chilly. Used for those sentenced by the Council of Ten, a major governing body of the Republic of Venice, they held people accused of political crimes and those serving short sentences. They were certainly bad enough, but worse in terms of comfort were the cells called the Pozzi, which means 'the wells'. They were damp, windowless cells on the ground floor of the palace and the only ventilation was through small holes in the thick stone walls. There was a wooden bucket with a lid in each cell for human excrement. It must have been a truly nightmarish situation to be locked up in there, indeed some prisoners scribbled desperate messages on the walls, pleading for freedom and these are still visible today. The New Prisons, which were built at the beginning of the 17th century, were of a better standard than both the Piombi and the Pozzi. They were connected to the old prisons by the small, covered Bridge of Sighs, so-called to emphasis the sadness of those prisoners who, having received their sentences in the palace courtroom, had to cross the bridge before entering the prison. Visitors on a tour of the palace can follow in their footsteps, though unlike the prisoners, they can come out again.

Serial seducer and man of action Casanova was imprisoned here because his philandering behaviour was considered depraved. He was also a suspected practitioner of the black arts and regarded as a fake who befriended elderly nobles, duping them with his faux magical knowledge. He was imprisoned for five years but before then decided enough was enough and made a harrowing but, it has to be said, clever escape. He climbed out through the roof, lowered himself down into the courtyard of the palace and simply walked out, straight to freedom. How cheeky is that?

The palace's main entrance, the Porta della Carta which when translated means the 'paper gate' lies between the Doge's Palace and the Basilica of San Marco. Theories as to why it was given this name are that either the state archives were housed here or that this was the gate where written requests to the government were submitted.

The interior of the palace is all swag and glamour, grand in the extreme and ornately furnished with enormously expensive art all over the place and intricate gilded ceilings. Unlike most museums, which is the function of the building today, paintings and sculptures were created especially for the palace, not collected or donated and added later. Major highlights for visitors to marvel at on a tour include Tintoretto's painting 'Paradise', one of the world's largest oil paintings, which covers a wall in the Council Hall.

Since 1996 the Doge's Palace has been part of the Venetian museums network, which has been under the management of the Fondazione Musei Civici di Venezia since 2008.

Interesting facts about the Doge's Palace:

• There was an art theft in the palace in October 1991. A guy called Vincenzo Pipino hid in a cell after dropping out of a tour group. He crossed the Bridge of Sighs in the middle of the night to the Sala di Censori where he stole a painting of the Madonna and child. By the next morning, the 16th-century work of art was in the possession of the Mala del Brenta organised crime group. Fortunately, it was recovered by police in November 1991.

• A silver book in the Scrigno Room was once used to register the city's noble families. Venice had a rigid class system formalised in the 16th century by laws that forbade marriage between nobles and commoners.

• Visitors can see the inner courtyard with its grand staircase flanked by statues of gods Mars and Neptune. It was the thing for the doge to meet visiting dignitaries at the bottom of the stairs, so that he could first descend in style from the top. This was a sign of his importance.

Address: Doge's Palace, San Marco, 1 30135 Venice

Website: http://palazzoducale.visitmuve.it/en/home/

Visitor information: The palace is open all year. Most areas are accessible to wheelchair users and there are accessible ground floor toilets. There is an on-site café and events and exhibitions are held regularly. Tours are available, although it is sensible to book tickets beforehand to avoid lengthy queues. Visitors can choose from normal or themed tours which include the Symbol of the City tour and the Doge's Hidden Treasures tour. There are also kid-friendly tours, workshops and treasure hunts.

– POLAND –

MALBORK CASTLE, MALBORK

Arguably the world's biggest castle and certainly the largest red-brick example, the beautifully preserved Malbork Castle hugs the banks of the river Nogat in northern Poland.

This UNESCO-listed structure is Europe's largest Gothic castle, a supersize fortress built in the style of the Teutonic Order of Knights of St Mary's Hospital in Jerusalem. The Teutonic Knights were a powerful order of 13th-century German crusaders and were sent to the area by the pope with the aim of converting the locals to Christianity. Malbork was originally called Marienburg, which means Mary's Castle, named after the Virgin Mary, the Order's patron saint.

Several times throughout its history, the castle was enlarged to accommodate a growing number of knights. At one time around 3,000 lived there. The complex consists of three separate parts: the High and Middle Castles and the Outer Bailey, and each section is separated by a huge dry moat. The outer wall encloses an area of 52 acres, which makes it around four times the size of Windsor Castle. That's huge.

This mighty medieval pile has look-at-me interiors. One of the most important is the Grand Refectory, the largest of all reception halls in the castle in medieval days. Its ceiling is held up by pillars shaped like palm trees. If you look closely you will also see a hole in a wall which was made by a cannonball centuries ago. Visitors can also view the central heating – a very clever system and extremely rare in medieval times.

The castle was captured by the Poles in the 1400s after it was taken by a group of crusaders who called themselves Teutonic mercenaries, in payment of debt. The Poles had spent a lot of time trying to get it back and after succeeding, they decided to make changes. The High Castle was converted from a monastery to a storage area for food, tar and – most importantly in the day – barrels of beer. Food supplies would include honey, fat, meat, butter and salt. Clerical staff and some military people took over the Middle Castle while the Outer or Lower Castle was used for defensive purposes. However, the building gradually began to suffer from neglect due to the significant cost of upkeep.

In 1772 the Prussians happened along and captured it. They moved into the High Castle but there were so many of them that it was deemed too small for their needs so they started to extend it. Thirty years later the transformation was complete. Medieval windows were bricked up and wooden roofs installed. However, in 1883 it was probably just as well that a decree was issued to prevent further destruction of the medieval structure.

During the Second World War part of the castle was badly damaged during a battle which raged for weeks between the Soviets and Germans. After the war ended, the idea was bandied about that it might be better to demolish what was left of the structure. Sense prevailed though – after all, though much of it was no more, there was still a substantial part of it that stood strong. It was reconstructed using detailed documentation from earlier conservationists.

It was not until 1961 that the newly created Castle Museum became the responsibility of the Polish government's Ministry of Culture and National Heritage. Among other things, it held one of Europe's largest collections of medieval architectural items. Today visitors can spend hours looking at items housed in the museum, it's stuffed with chivalric imagery from around 700 items in the amber collection and rooms full of antique statues, works of art and jewellery to medals, coins, banknotes, purses, sacks and scales for weighing gold coins. Ceramics? Yes, of course. The ceramics collection ranges from the Middle Ages to the 20th century and includes Delft items. Furniture? Absolutely. Everything from Gothic to more modern items. The oldest items date back to the 14th century, when the Teutonic Knights were in residence.

For visitors on a tour of the castle, they will see the *danske* – the toilet tower used by the knights, which is connected to the castle by a walkway. Interestingly, it is said they used cabbage leaves for toilet paper! Look for the medieval carving of a little devil who indicates the way to the toilet. It seems these medieval knights had a sense of humour …

Interesting facts about Malbork Castle:

• The castle, which lies 82 kilometres from Gdańsk and 315 kilometres from Warsaw, is one of the country's biggest tourist attractions.

• Malbork Castle is the greatest fortification built by medieval knights during the Baltic Crusades.

• A re-enactment of the Siege of Malbork takes place every July. Alongside this are displays of medieval and puppet theatre, painting workshops, jugglers, stilt walkers and fire eaters.

Address: Malbork Castle, Starościńska 1, 82-200 Malbork

Website: http://zamek.malbork.pl

Photo: DerHexer

Visitor information: Open daily with free entry on Mondays, but visitors must purchase an audio guide. It is easy to spend a whole day at the castle to see all it has to offer. It makes sense to wear comfortable shoes and arrive in the morning to have time to get a good look at everything.

There are frequent evening light and sound performances held in the courtyards and night tours of the interior of the castle in both winter and summer. The castle hosts regular music concerts, medieval-style banquets and knights' tournaments.

A restaurant in the grounds offers refreshments and there are shops too.

– PORTUGAL –

MATEUS PALACE, VILLA REAL

If you are of a certain age and can remember the 1970s, perhaps you recall the flask-shaped bottles of Mateus rosé wine that were a staple of the time. This is the palace which is still depicted on bottle labels.

Mateus Palace was built for the Third Morgado de Mateus, António José Botelho Mourão, just outside the town of Vila Real which in English translates as 'Royal Town'. It was founded by King Denis of Portugal during the Middle Ages.

The palace was designed and built by Italian-born visionary architect and artist, Nicolau Nasoni. He obviously did a good job as it is considered to be one of Portugal's finest examples of baroque architecture. It oozes opulence, from its elegant exterior festooned with gold-leaf detailing to its interior halls brimming with silverware and ceramics, some of which date back to the 16th century.

The palace has entrancing baroque entrance stairways while the roof is crowned with obelisks. Intricately carved wood ceilings and dark chestnut wooden floors and rugs from different time periods grace the rooms, together with gorgeous examples of 16th-, 17th- and 18th-century Portuguese, British and French furniture. There is a spectacular library which contains rare first editions including Luís Vaz de Camões' 'Os Lusíadas', an epic poem which is a cornerstone of Portuguese patriotism. Another room holds an eclectic collection of religious bric-a-brac, including three dozen rather macabre 18th-century relics from the Vatican. These include a piece of holy fingernail, a saintly set of eyeballs and a piece of the cross – each with the Vatican's proof of authenticity. Presumably they came to Mateus by way of architect Nasoni.

Within the palace itself, several wings exhibit historic artefacts from heritage sites throughout the Douro Valley and beyond. One of the most fascinating of these exhibition spaces is the Sacred Art Room, which houses a collection of primitive religious artworks.

The chapel, built in 1750, has a baroque façade and hand-painted tiles. Inside visitors can see an exquisite set of priest's robes embroidered with gold and silver thread while in a side apse lies the mummified body of a 4th-century soldier who was beheaded.

While the interior is outstanding, even more so are the elaborate gardens created in the 20th century, which were modelled on Versailles. Surrounded by vineyards, there is a fabulous 100-foot-long walk through a fragrant tunnel of cedar trees, it's a welcome respite from the summer heat.

Photo: François Philipp

Dotted around are boxwood hedges, statues and ponds while a collection of fanciful, tall curved ladders used to prune the tunnel's exterior branches catch the eye.

But to get back to the wine itself, Mateus rosé. There is a small vineyard and winery in the grounds but they make port wine, not Mateus. You can also purchase port wine, though not Mateus wine in the gift shop. Strange? Yes, in a way, but this is because despite the palace gracing the label, it never had much to do with the wine itself. During the Second World War, a new Portuguese wine company was created by a group of people because there was a huge surplus of grapes in the Douro Valley. The people in question rented a winery from a cooperative but really didn't know much about wine production. Anyway, they produced a red wine called 'Vila Real' and a white called 'Cambriz'. They tried their hand at producing rosé but in the beginning it didn't work well. They joined forces with a French winemaker and voilà, a rosé was born. What would they call it though? Not far from the winery in Vila Real there was a rather splendid baroque palace. Ah, that would look good on the label, they thought. At the time, the palace belonged to the Duke of Mangualde and, after discussion, the partners offered a commission of 50 centavos (0.5 escudo) a bottle or a fixed sum in exchange for the use of the name of the property. They eventually agreed on a contract where they bought grapes from the estate at a 30 per cent premium. The wine was christened Mateus. The company, now called Sogrape, is Portugal's largest wine producer.

Interesting facts about Mateus Palace:

• In 1971 the palace became a private foundation and is now the venue for music concerts, art exhibitions and literary prize-giving awards.

• In its heyday, Mateus rosé was a favoured tipple of many rich and famous folks including, so it is said, HM Queen Elizabeth II and Sir Cliff Richard. It became the trendy drink in the 1970s when Jimi Hendrix was photographed drinking it out of a bottle and Elton John sang about it in his 1973 song 'Social Disease'. It even had a part in a film too, *Animal House*, (1978) in the home of Professor Dave Jennings, played by Donald Sutherland.

• Mateus rosé's unique bottle design was based on a Portuguese water flask used by soldiers during the Great War.

Address: Mateus Palace, Fundação da Casa de Mateus, Casa de Mateus, 5000-291 Vila Real

Website: www.casademateus.com

Visitor information: Guided tours (in English, French, Spanish and German) take visitors through the main quarters and the garden.

– ROMANIA –

BRAN CASTLE, BRAN

We all know Transylvania is the home of bloodthirsty vampires. Could there be a more fitting location for creepy Bran Castle than atop craggy peaks in a wild region of the Carpathian Mountains?

Originally a military fortress perched 762 metres high (2,500 feet) on a cliff on the Transylvania–Wallachia border, the building was completed in 1388 and in subsequent years saw Saxons, Teutonic Knights, Romanian royalty and military regiments come and go. Between 1438 and 1442 it was used in defence against the Ottoman Empire and later became a customs post on the mountain pass.

Bram Stoker became world famous as the creator of the most famous vampire ever to exist in the world of the living dead, the Transylvanian Count Dracula, Prince of Darkness. Most people erroneously think of Bran Castle as Dracula's Castle. However, it has little or no connection to either Bram Stoker's fictional vampire or ruler Vlad Tepes. Better known as 'Vlad the Impaler', who Stoker's Dracula is said to be loosely based on, Tepes ordered the brutal torture of tens of thousands of people in the 15th century.

This 14th-century fortress is actually one of several castles linked to the *Dracula* legend and there is no evidence that author Stoker knew anything at all about this particular castle. He didn't visit the area and his description of Dracula's crumbling fictional castle bears no resemblance to Bran Castle. Although he set his chilling novel in Transylvania much of his inspiration was drawn from a coastal area in the north-east of Scotland, a few miles south of Peterhead to be precise, where he was entranced by the sight of the sinister and brooding Slains Castle, perched on a steep cliff top, reaching into the sky like a mysterious sentinel overlooking the inhospitable North Sea.

Fast forward to 1920 and Bran became a royal residence within the Kingdom of Romania. It was Queen Marie's favourite home and retreat and she oversaw extensive renovations conducted by Czech architect Karel Zdeněk Líman. After her death, the castle was inherited by her daughter Princess Ileana who ran a hospital there in the Second World War. Later it was seized by the communist regime, which meant the expulsion of the royal family in 1948. That was when the castle was turned into a government-run museum.

But often right prevails and on 18 May 2009, after 61 years, four months and eleven days of state ownership, the administration of Bran Castle was transferred from the government to the remaining children of Princess Ileana of Romania. Inside the castle, all traces of the family had been eliminated and what once was Queen Marie's most cherished residence and a family home was stripped bare. The family opted to reopen it as the first private museum in Romania.

The castle was already one of Romania's top tourist destinations and now the museum, dedicated to displaying art and furniture collected by Queen Marie, sees over 500,000 visitors each year.

Interesting facts about Bran Castle:

• Winding stairways lead through 60 timbered rooms, many also connected by underground passages.

• Rooms house collections of furniture, weapons and armour dating from the 14th–19th centuries chosen by Queen Marie. Throughout the castle, hand-carved fixtures adorn the walls and ceilings.

• A footnote about Bram Stoker. His friendship with Arminius Vámbéry, a professor of eastern languages at the University of Budapest, was the spur for him to start writing his own tale of a vampire. Vámbéry told Stoker the story of the real-life Dracula, cruel Vlad Dracula Tepes, prince of

Photo: Snowkiie.ro

Wallachia, an ancient kingdom now part of Romania. Born in 1431 Vlad was a sadistic figure in Romanian history. His surname 'Tepes' translates as 'the impaler' and 'Dracul' means 'devil' or 'dragon'.

Address: Bran Castle, Strada General Traian Moșoiu 24, Bran 507025

Website: www.bran-castle.com

Visitor information: Regular events take place in the grounds including medieval tournaments, music festivals, children's pageants, jazz concerts and food fairs. Recognising Bram Stoker's novel, *Dracula*, visitors can also see rooms dedicated to Transylvania's most famous count. At the time of writing, there are plans to install a glass lift to experience Dracula's 'escape route'. Of course, as would be expected there are Halloween celebrations here too. Tourists can wander round the interior on their own or take a guided tour.

– RUSSIA –

PETERHOF PALACE, ST PETERSBURG

St Petersburg itself is not short of palaces, but around 30 miles away on the coast of the Gulf of Finland, lies Peterhof, one of Russia's most spectacular.

Sometimes referred to as the 'Russian Versailles' or the

'capital of fountains', Peter the Great had the palace complex built as his glorious residence by the sea, though in truth he preferred the modest Monplaisir Palace, part of the Peterhof complex, to the main imperial palace.

Peterhof is actually three palaces, of which the Grand Palace is the best known and most impressive. Indeed, if the word had been around at the time, it would have been called 'blingy'. The palaces, gardens and town centre are recognised as a UNESCO World Heritage Site.

The Grand Palace was inspired by Tsar Peter the Great's visit to Versailles in 1717. His original plan was to build a palace further to the east at Strelna, but his plans were thwarted by the boggy terrain. It was totally unsuitable for the canals and fountains he had in mind so he abandoned that idea. However, a few years earlier work had begun on a modest structure on the current site and a small palace was completed in 1721.

At the same time a great deal of work was underway to create the Lower Park and the sea canal as well as Monplaisir, originally built for the Tsar's wife Catherine I. This became a family home. The Marly Palace, also on the site, was again inspired by Peter the Great's visit to France and based on Louis XIV's hunting lodge at Marly-le-Roi, built as an intimate alternative to Versailles.

As time passed, the original palace was viewed as too small for the setting so the Tsar instructed architects to create something bigger and grander. However, he died in 1725 and thereafter little work was done on the site until 1740 when Peter's daughter, Elizabeth, came to the throne. Bartolomeo Rastrelli, who was responsible for the massive reconstruction of the Winter Palace in St Petersburg, was asked to create a new Summer Palace on the site.

The current palace is around 300 metres long and stands on a sixteen-metre-high ridge that marks the border between

Photo: © Gilly Pickup

the Upper and Lower parks. It was built around the end of the baroque period. While symmetrical and classically straightforward on the outside and indeed long, it is quite narrow. The interior, with around 30 rooms, is however far more eye catching.

The Chesma Hall holds a number of paintings depicting the Battle of Chesma: a naval encounter in the war of 1768–74 between Russia and Turkey. They are by German artist Jacob Hackert, who was initially criticised for his poor depiction of exploding ships. Well, after all, Hackert had never seen one. It is rumoured that Catherine II – the feisty Catherine the Great (incidentally, her name wasn't Catherine at all, it was Sophie), blew up a ship in Livorno for him to see, so he could make appropriate alterations to the paintings.

Other outstanding items include the magnificent ceremonial staircase, richly decorated ballroom and splendid throne room. There is also a significant Chinese influence, with Chinese cabinets decorated in black and yellow lacquer landscapes looking resplendent in the Chesma Hall. In comparison, the Tsar's oak study is relatively simple. Oak panels lining the walls were designed by French sculptor Pineau. The room and furnishings are all wood, except the white-marble fireplace with a long mirror framed in carved oak which hangs above the mantelpiece. The room also contains Peter the Great's table clock in a rectangular case of gilt bronze.

The broad façade of the Grand Palace overlooks a terrace, Upper Garden and the Grand Cascade, which has the appearance of a sequence of huge, beautifully decorated steps with an endless series of large gilded statues and fountains.

The Grand Cascade leads to the Sea Channel, one of the baroque period's largest water constructions which divides the Lower Gardens. These gardens, based upon formal French gardens of the time, are extensive. Fountains are a major component here with over twenty named ones as well as numerous un-named ones. It's interesting how they operate – water from natural springs is collected in the upper gardens and piped to the fountains below. They are thus fed by gravity and no pumps are used, though this does restrict the hours of usage.

Visitors today can wander the Lower Park, where Monplaisir is located, the Upper Garden with the great Neptune Fountain, the Grand Cascade and the main palace.

Interesting facts about Peterhof Palace:

• During the Second World War Peterhof was one of many places captured by the German army and staff were only partially successful in saving the palace's treasures; many structural elements were destroyed. However, immediately after the end of local hostilities in 1944, restoration work began and the lower gardens were re-opened in 1945.

• In view of anti-German feelings, Peterhof was re-named Petrodvorets, but it reverted to Peterhof in 1997. Clearly the restoration has been a magnificent achievement and while some work may continue, it is one of the most stunning palaces and gardens you are likely to see.

• In a further link to modern times, in 1721 Peter the Great also founded the adjacent Peterhof Fabric, later renamed the Petrodvorets watch factory. In the 1960s it started producing Raketa brand watches in honour of Yuri Gagarin, Russian astronaut and the first man in space. Visitors can go to the company today and buy the watches.

Address: Peterhof Palace, Razvodnaya Ulitsa, 2, St Petersburg

Website: http://en.peterhofmuseum.ru

Visitor information: A visit to the palace is an easy side trip from St Petersburg.

When visiting don't miss the Chinese Study Rooms decorated with ornate motifs and black lacquer panels. The Great Palace is open daily except Mondays and the last Tuesday of each month.

– SLOVENIA –

PREDJAMA CASTLE, PREDJAMA

There's no denying it. Predjama Castle, perched halfway up a 123-metre high cliff, is a dramatic landmark. Dominating the area for more than 800 years, the bold structure is listed in the Guinness Book of World Records as the world's largest cave castle.

Yes, this is a castle partly built inside a cave, how clever is that? Originally called Jama Castle - *jama* translated means 'cave' – the natural cave walls and man-made castle are so inextricably linked it is well-nigh impossible to figure out where one begins and the other ends.

In 1478 the fortress became the property of a knight and robber baron called Erazem Lueger. According to legend, in 1483 he killed Marshall Pappenheim at the Vienna Court during an argument in which Pappenheim had offended the honour of Erazem's friend. However, Pappenheim was somebody Erazem shouldn't really have messed with because he was a relative of Holy Roman Emperor Frederick III. As soon as he realised what he had done, the robber baron Erazem fled to Predjama to escape punishment. Frederick's forces came after him and forced him into hiding in his castle. They thought he wouldn't last long in there without starving. They didn't reckon on Erazem's wiliness though and the fact there was a handy secret tunnel between the castle and a nearby cave. That meant he could replenish supplies quite easily from the town nearby without his enemies knowing.

When the Austrians tried to finish off both the castle and Erazem, he simply laughed at them. At one point, he threw buckets full of cherries at them, probably just to show that he was quite comfortable where he was. Erazem lived like this for a year and a day. It was really unfortunate therefore that after surviving for so long, one of his own servants betrayed him in a really nasty way. When the robber baron went to the toilet, which was on an outside parapet of the castle, the servant raised a flag and it only took a single shot from a cannon to blast Erazem off the toilet.

In 1567 Hans Kobenzl, an Austrian knight, bought the castle. He set to work on it, rebuilding here and enlarging there and it is mostly the result of this building campaign that is visible today. His descendants remained owners of the castle until 1810. After two more owners, the castle was confiscated by the state after the Second World War.

The castle is now a museum and visitors can see how people worked and lived there by taking a tour of the living areas, the chapel, torture chamber and dungeon. Audio guides alert guests to where to look to see holes in the entrance tower ceiling which were used for pouring boiling oil on intruders and there is a 16th-century chest

Photo: Avack

THE 50 GREATEST CASTLES AND PALACES OF THE WORLD

full of treasure which was unearthed in the cellar in 1991. Meanwhile objects on view include weapons: spears, bows, arrows and armour; oil paintings, and a Pietà dating from 1420. For those who don't know what a Pietà is, it's a painting or sculpture of Mary, holding the body of Jesus. Besides that, like all proper castles, it has a drawbridge over a fast flowing river, a spooky dungeon and even a hidey hole at the top called Erazem's Nook.

Steep wooden stairs lead visitors into the depths of the cave. There is a drinking water source here and you can see where the water drips down into a pipe, taking it through the walls and down into the castle's living area. From the castle, a passage leads to an observation post and a well on the rocky cliff and this is where to find the entrance to Erazem's Tunnel.

Every summer there is a medieval tournament in Erazem's memory which involves archers, swordsmen and horsemen. Merchants and craftsmen sell medieval products and there is entertainment in the form of dancers, magicians, puppet shows and musicians.

Interesting facts about Predjama Castle:

• It has been the location for some local feature films, while in 1986 it was one of the locations in the film *Armour of God*, which starred Jackie Chan.

• Predjama Castle is said to be haunted and some years ago a team from the Discovery Channel came to see if they could find any answers to spooky goings on. Although they managed to capture a number of strange shaped orbs and indistinct sounds, they came no closer to finding out who or what was involved. It was also investigated for paranormal activity in a 2008 episode of *Ghost Hunters International* on the Sci-Fi Channel.

• Predjama Castle was built in 1274 by the Patriarchs of Aquileia who named it in rough translation from the Latin 'Cave Castle in the Karst'; the castle's Slovene name, Predjamski Grad means 'Castle in front of the cave'. It was later rebuilt by new owners, the Luegg family.

Address: Predjama Castle, 6230 Predjama

Website: www.postojnska-jama.eu/en/come-and-visit-us

Visitor information: Visits are available year-round while between May and September it is also possible to explore the cave under Predjama Castle. Due to its location and favourable temperatures the cave is inhabited by a colony of bats, as a result of which visitors have no access to it during the bats' hibernation.

– SPAIN –

ROYAL PALACE OF MADRID, MADRID

The Royal Palace, or Palacio Real, is the official residence of the Spanish Royal Family. This was home to the kings of Spain from Charles III to Alfonso XIII and is now used mainly for ceremonial and public functions. The present Spanish royal family live in the more modest Palacio de la Zarzuela, on the outskirts of the city.

A 9th-century Moorish castle once stood here but it was burned down in 1734. In 1738, King Philip V, Spain's first king from the French house of Bourbon, constructed a new palace. It was built mainly from granite and colmenar stone and was completed in 1764. This is the late baroque palace that we see today although some room layouts have changed over the years as the building was adapted to suit its residents.

The palace, which has around 3,000 rooms, is built in the form of a square and looks out over a courtyard. It has a lavish interior and is awash with paintings by Velazquez, Goya and Caravaggio including his painting of Salome with the head of John the Baptist. There are frescoes too, by Giaquinto, Tiepolo and Mengs, and besides artwork, visitors can see collections of porcelain, watches, regal armoury, silverware and furniture.

The Music Museum attracts huge interest as it has two violins, a cello and a viola, gifts to King Felipe V in 1702 by Stradivarius. They are the only set of decorated instruments the great man is known to have made. The Library is another essential sight with one of the biggest collections of books, manuscripts, maps and musical scores in the world, while in the Throne Room visitors can see one of the palace's highlights – the thrones of King Juan Carlos and Queen Sofía. Then there's the Royal Dining Room, redesigned for King Alfonso XII in 1880 and still used for official banquets. It has an array of chandeliers that each hold 1,000 candles, a long table and masses of chairs. Those that the king and queen use are a little taller than the rest.

Visitors who like seeing suits of armour and frightening medieval torture implements will be in their element in the Royal Armoury, even the suits of armour worn by El Cid and his horse are there, displayed on statues. The armoury's impressive collection goes back to the 13th century and besides the above, includes powder flasks, shields, lances, helmets and saddles from Carlos V's collection.

That's not all there is to see here, if you add in the imposing collections of tapestries, table porcelain, gold and silver plates and clocks (something King Carlos IV was particularly passionate about), you have a palace with bags of pizazz.

The Farmacia Real, or Royal Pharmacy, is one of the oldest in Europe and contains medicine jars, stills for mixing royal concoctions, ceramic pots and prescriptions given to members of the royal family. Its purpose was to bring relief from illnesses suffered by the Spanish royals over the centuries.

There is plenty to see outside too. The palace is surrounded by parks and gardens, including the neo classically-styled Sabatini Gardens with a large pond surrounded by fountains. Limestone statues of kings were originally intended to crown the roof of the palace, but it was decided that they would be too heavy and that it was better to leave them on the ground. Sensible decision.

Interesting facts about the Royal Palace of Madrid:

• The last time the palace was used for a royal ceremony was in 2004 when Prince Felipe, now the king, and Letizia Ortiz were married in the central courtyard.

• The palace has 135,000 square metres (1,450,000 square feet) of floor space and is Europe's largest royal palace by floor area. It has 870 windows, 240 balconies, 44 staircases and the main staircase has 70 steps.

• In October 2017 the enormous royal kitchen was opened to the public after major renovations. Visitors can ponder over many interesting pieces of kitchenware used over the centuries including royal paella pans.

Address: Royal Palace of Madrid, Calle de Bailén, s/n, 28071 Madrid

Website: www.patrimonionacional.es/

Visitor information: Some of the palace's rooms are open to the public and these include the Dining Room, Throne Room, Royal Pharmacy, Royal Armoury and banqueting halls. Once inside visitors have to keep to a stated route, but do not have to follow a tour. Guided tours take place regularly and the palace is open except when there are official ceremonies. Disabled access and manual wheelchairs are available. Photography is allowed inside in certain areas, but no flash. In the courtyard, the ceremonial changing of the guard in full parade dress takes place at noon on the first Wednesday of every month except during August and September and is free to the public. A less grand ceremony takes place in the palace compound at the Puerta del Príncipe every Wednesday.

– SWEDEN –

STOCKHOLM PALACE, STOCKHOLM

Stockholm Palace is the Swedish monarch's official residence, although the royal family's private home is Drottningholm Palace on Lovön Island, formerly a summer residence for the Royal Court.

The royal palace is not only the monarch's official residence, it is also the workplace for the king, queen and various departments of the royal court. The combination of official residence, place of work and historic monument gives Stockholm Palace unique appeal.

The site of the palace dates back to the mid-13th century and was once where the huge Tre Kronor Castle (Three Crowns) stood, so-called after three crowns which topped the tower. It burned down in 1697 with only the north wing of the castle escaping severe damage.

A new palace was planned for the site and work started the following year. However, great expense elsewhere was incurred due to the Northern War and work on the palace was suspended. In the end, it took 60 years to complete, although initially it was expected to take only five. After the renovations it had 600-plus rooms spread across seven floors, with four façades representing the king (west façade), the queen (east), the nation (south) and royalty in general (north).

In the late 1750s King Adolf Frederick and Queen Louisa Ulrika took up residence in the now baroque-style palace. Incidentally, King Adolf is known as the king who ate himself to death. Literally. On 12 February 1771, which was Shrove Tuesday, he prepared himself for Lent by eating all the food he would have to forego during the season. So, he sat down to large platefuls of lobster, caviar, kippers, sauerkraut and boiled meat. It wasn't unusual for him to eat a lot, he often did, but that day he went over the top. He drank lots of champagne and then ate *semlas* (Swedish sweet buns) for pudding. He didn't just eat one or two or even three – no, he ate fourteen. He must have felt awful after eating that lot and later that day he died from digestive problems.

Inside the palace there are numerous visitor attractions. The royal apartments, which have the oldest interiors in the

Photo: Jorge Láscar

palace, include rooms used for state occasions and royal receptions. There is a spectacular ballroom called 'The White Sea' and a Hall of State with Queen Christina's magnificent silver throne which was created for her coronation in 1650.

The apartments of the Orders of Chivalry house a collection of regal honours while the banqueting hall is used for major dining events. There are guest apartments where visiting heads of state and similar dignitaries stay. When Gustav III lived in these apartments – he was a son of King Adolf Frederick and Queen Louisa Ulrika – he sent out invitations to Swedish noblemen to watch him wake up in the morning. For some reason they were hugely sought after at the time. Talking of Gustav III, a Museum of Antiquities in the palace is dedicated to him. It opened in 1794 and is one of Europe's oldest museums. He was a fan of art and antiquities and collected a number of sculptures when he visited Italy at the end of the 18th century. After his death it was decided that the collection of over 200 sculptures would be put on public view.

The smaller Bernadotte Rooms are used for more intimate events such as the presentation of awards, medals and investitures of foreign ambassadors. The Treasury, home to the royal regalia, is in the palace vaults. It was only set up in 1970 and before that the regalia was kept locked away and hidden from public view. Erik XIV's crown, sceptre and orb, used at his coronation in 1561, are here, as is a sword of state which belonged to his father Gustav Vasa. On show too is Louisa Ulrika's crown. It is a fabulous thing, made in 1751 and crafted in silver with a staggering 695 diamonds! It must have felt extremely heavy when she wore it. Nowadays that wouldn't be a problem because, in Sweden, a crown is no longer placed on the monarch's head at their coronation, but placed symbolically on a chair beside them. Visitors can see Maria Eleonora's crown too, made in 1620 and weighing 2.5 kilograms (5.5 pounds), and the coronation cloak of King Oscar II, the last king of Sweden who was actually crowned. The Treasury also holds the silver royal font, which dates back to 1696 and is still used for royal baptisms. The Bernadotte Library contains the royal book collection with approximately 100,000 books and half a million photographs.

Celebrating the original structure, the Tre Kronor Museum is in the north wing. This was the area that suffered least damage in the 1697 fire and there are objects on view dating from that time. Visitors enter through a door in its defensive wall which dates back to the 13th century and is five metres (sixteen feet) thick.

The Livrustkammaren, founded in 1633, is a royal armoury and Sweden's oldest museum. Its impressive collection of state coaches, royal clothes and armoury is in the basement of the palace's east wing. This is where to see the costume worn by Gustav III at the masked ball where he was assassinated in 1792. There is also a stuffed horse called Streiff which was ridden by Gustav II Adolf when he was killed in battle in 1632. Seekers of the gruesome might like to ponder over the glass jar that contains the stomach contents of one of the conspirators of Gustav III's assassination.

Interesting facts about Stockholm Palace:

• Gustav III's assassination inspired Verdi to write the opera *The Masked Ball.*

• Some reports say there are now 1,430 rooms in the palace, of which 660 have windows. I can't imagine the job of having to record them all!

• The palace's outer courtyard is popular with tourists who want to see the spectacle of the changing of the guard. Every year nearly 1 million visitors come to witness this. There have been royal guards at the palace since 1523 and during the summer, dressed in their striking blue uniform and accompanied by a military band, they march through the nearby streets.

Address: Stockholm Palace, Slottsbacken 1, Old Town (Gamla Stan)

Website: www.kungligaslotten.se/english/royal-palaces-and-sites/the-royal-palace.html

Visitor information: Prams are not permitted in the palace but can be parked outside. Visitors can photograph and film for private use as long as it does not disturb other visitors, guided tours, or other activity at the palace.

The Royal Chapel functions as a parish church and hosts organ concerts in summer.

Children love the free-entry playroom in the Livrustkammaren where they can try on knight costumes and princess dresses, play, read and draw.

– SWITZERLAND –

CHÂTEAU DE CHILLON, VEYTAUX

Set against the peaks of the Savoy mountains on an island in Lake Geneva, the site of Chillon Castle has supported a settlement since the Bronze Age.

Lord Byron was so stirred by the Château de Chillon that he carved his name on a pillar in the dungeon. In a letter to John Murray, his publisher, he said: 'Clarens and Vevey and the Château de Chillon are places of which I shall say little because all I could say must fall short of the impressions they stamp.' Byron also penned a poem, 'The Prisoner of Chillon', about a monk called François de Bonivard who was imprisoned in the castle dungeon for four years – or six years, depending on which source you believe – for supporting the Reformation. These days graffiti is frowned upon and rightly so, but Byron had no such qualms when he painstakingly scratched his name into the stonework of the castle. It's still there and popular with tourists, though it is protected by a Perspex covering.

The first written mention of the castle was in 1150 when the Counts of Savoy controlled the fort and surrounding area. From the 13th century onwards the castle was extended and under Pierre II of Savoy became their summer residence. Its location made it an attractive place to go for the holidays but since it wasn't occupied all year round, it began to fall into disrepair and eventually became nothing more than an empty shell used as a prison. The Bernese, who didn't get on with the Savoys, besieged what was left of the building in 1536, and the Savoys fled through a secret door in the dungeon to safety. That was that – the Bernese kept hold of the castle for the next 200 years, though like the Savoys before them used it mainly as a prison and somewhere to store their weapons.

After that, there was more bickering when the Vaudois fell out with the Bernese and in 1803 the castle became the property of the Canton of Vaud.

The layout of the castle is interesting as the side facing the mainland is primed for defence with arrow slits and

Photo: VeerayaVSK

battlements while the side overlooking the lake has a graceful, fortification-free façade. Back in medieval times the castle must have been exceedingly modern as it had a regular supply of fresh water from the lake, a luxury not readily available to most in those days.

There are three great tapestry-draped halls – the Aula Magna, Castellan's dining hall and the Domus Clericorum. Back in the day, they would have been the setting for fantastic banquets or used as places to dole out justice. Visitors can see the decorated window seats, which were originally seating-places for ladies to sew in the light, while some toilets in the chambers of the Duke of Savoy and later Castellans of Bern are decorated with crude medieval art. Talking of toilets, there are several medieval garderobes on the castle's lake-facing side which opened out onto the water below. It may seem strange to us nowadays that some of these toilets were designed for two people!

But let us go back for a moment to Lord Byron, after all, the castle's fame is due in part to his visit during the rainy summer of 1816. His companions were his mistress Claire Claremont and her stepsister Mary Godwin, his doctor, John Polidori and Mary's lover, Percy Shelley. Perhaps it was a sign of boredom, but they decided to see which one of them could write the best, i.e. scariest, horror story. Shelley came up with 'Fragment of a Ghost Story', Byron wrote 'The Vampyre' and young Mary Godwin, who later married Percy Shelley, wrote what would become the most famous and fearsome of all tales of horror – she created 'Frankenstein'.

Interesting facts about the Château de Chillon:

• Henry James set his novella *Daisy Miller* here and Jean-Jacques Rousseau included the castle in his novel *La Nouvelle Heloise.*

• The castle courtyards were the site of numerous torturings and burnings of suspected witches at the end of the 16th century.

• Visitors can see 14th-century frescoes both in the Count's room and in the chapel, as well as underground vaults, the Great Halls and ancient weapons.

Address: Château de Chillon, Avenue de Chillon 21, 1820 Veytaux

Website: www.chillon.ch/en

Visitor information: The castle is open daily and guided tours are available by reservation, made at least two working days ahead. Visitors can explore by themselves if they don't want a formal tour. A pamphlet gives suggestions for a route that winds in and out of the building. Audio guides are available in various languages. There is a picnic area in the grounds.

The castle is also a popular place to hold a reception or special event, with lots of family activities taking place in the castle and grounds throughout the year. These include holiday workshops, birthday parties, a museum night and a creepy 'night of horror', sure to be nerve-jangling enough to enthral your little terrors. Children can have fun romping around and exploring the castle's nooks and crannies.

– TURKEY –

TOPKAPI PALACE, ISTANBUL

With a spectacular setting overlooking the Bosphorus and the Sea of Marmara, Topkapi Palace was a royal residence for around 400 years until the collapse of the Ottoman Empire in the 1920s. The vast palace occupies an area of 700,000 square metres.

In 1460 Mehmed the Conqueror set about organising the building of Topkapi Palace after he conquered Constantinople, the city we know as Istanbul. As you'd expect, much work was involved and it took eighteen years to complete. It served as the Palace for the Ottoman sultans across the centuries until 1856 when Sultan Abdulmejid I decided to move the court to the newer Dolmabahçe Palace. Topkapi retained a number of functions including the Treasury and the Mint.

The courtyards of Topkapi are linked by passages. The main entrance, the imposing Imperial Gate, leads to the first courtyard, the Courtyard of Regiments. Only the sultan could cross this gate on horseback, everyone else had to walk. This area contained the Church of Hagia Irene which was used as the Armoury as well as the Mint and Hospital.

The second gate, the Gate of Salutation, was so named because everyone passing through had to salute the sultan. This led to the Divan Square or Square of Justice and also to the Harem. The literal meaning of the word 'Harem' is 'forbidden' in Arabic, and at Topkapi, these were lavish apartments where sultans lived with their wives, concubines, sisters, brothers, mother and children under the fierce protection of the black eunuchs. Expanded over the centuries by each sultan, today the Topkapi Palace Harem has around 300 rooms, including nine bathrooms, two mosques, a hospital and a laundry.

The third courtyard and gate, the Gate of Felicitation leads to the Inner Palace, the sultan's private area. It contained the Hall of Audience and the Throne Room, where the sultan would meet ambassadors and dignitaries. For security reasons, those working in this area were chosen from the local deaf and mute community.

The Privy Room in the inner courtyard contains holy items sent to the sultan over a period dating back to 1517, while the Pavilion of the Holy Mantle holds Mohmmed's cloak, sword, teeth and beard. These relics are known as the Sacred Trusts. Even the sultan and his family were permitted entrance here only once a year, on the 15th day of Ramadan, when the Palace was a residence. Now visitors can see these items any day of the year and many Muslims come on pilgrimage for this purpose.

The fourth courtyard, known as the Imperial Sofa, was a private area with gardens and terraces where the sultans could chill, had that word been around at the time.

When the Ottoman Empire ended in 1923 the palace became a state-owned museum. While there are hundreds of rooms, only a few are now open to the public, including the Harem and Treasury.

The museum's weapons collection is one of the world's finest, with over 50,000 items. There is also a fine collection of paintings here for visitors to see, including those of the 36 sultans right from the beginning of the Ottoman Empire in 1299. The first sultan to commission a portrait was Mehmed II, the 7th Sultan, so previous paintings must have been based either on historic descriptions or imagination.

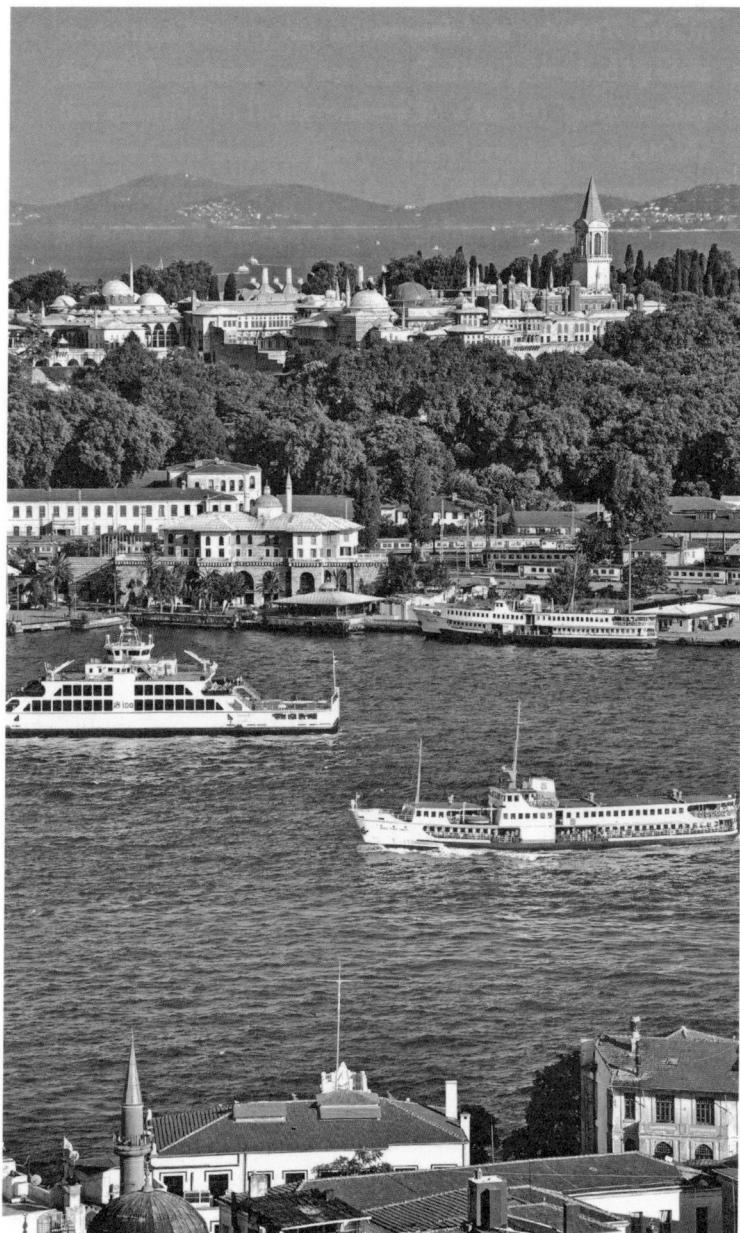

Photo: Moonik

There is a collection of 16th- to 19th-century silverware too.

The kitchens, including a confectionery kitchen, creamery and rooms for the cooks were the largest in the Ottoman Empire. They contain a spectacular collection of Chinese porcelain, the largest outside China. Items range from the late Sung (13th century) and the Yuan dynasties (1280–1368), through the Ming (1368–1644) to the Ch'ing period (1644–1912). More than 800 kitchen staff were employed here at any one time with this number rising to 1,000 on religious holidays such as Ramadan.

The Confectionery House has a collection of copper items and tombac ware first used in the 16th century. Tombac was produced by applying an alloy of gold and mercury to the copper, which resulted in a golden lustre finish. The kitchens catered for up to 5,000 occupants of the palace at any one time. A sample menu from Topkapi during Ramadan would have been:

Starters
- *Hoşaf* (a stewed fruit compote)
- *Şerbet* (a traditional nectar)
- *Yufka* (filo pastry with an assortment of fillings)
- Bread, olives, cheeses, cold cuts

Main meal
- Soups
- Meat dishes – one favourite was fried eggs with cured spiced beef and onions

Desserts
- Pastry-oriented, the most traditional Ramadan dessert being *Güllaç*: layers of thin corn starch pastry soaked in rosewater-infused milk.

The Treasury houses priceless items of art and jewellery from around the world, some made for the sultan, others given as presents. Star of the show is the 86-carat Spoonmaker's Diamond, set in silver and surrounded by a double row of 49 old-mine-cut diamonds. It is one of the world's most famous diamonds. Other fascinating items include an emerald-encrusted dagger and a diamond-studded quiver and bow.

Interesting facts about Topkapi Palace:

• In 1964 a film entitled *Topkapi*, based on the novel *The Light of Day* was released telling the story of how a gang of crooks planned to steal the highly-prized item, the emerald-encrusted dagger. The cast included stars of the day such as Melina Mercouri, Peter Ustinov and Maximilian Schell. In 1965 Peter Ustinov won the Oscar for Best Supporting Actor for his role and the Golden Laurel award for the same category.

• Worth seeing is the Privy Chamber of Murat III. Its blue, white and coral 16th-century Iznik-tiled walls cosset an indoor pool and gilded fireplace.

• Ottoman sultans dedicated days for breaking fast with their wives and loved ones and had specific areas constructed for this purpose. Sultan Ibrahim I had an alcove built in the palace garden so that he could breakfast in private with his wife.

Address: Topkapi Palace, Cankurtaran Mh., 34122 Fatih/ Istanbul

Website: http://topkapisarayi.gov.tr/en

Visitor information: Annual visitors: 3,335,000.

The museum is open to the public every day except Tuesdays, but there may be restrictions during Ramadan. Photography in exhibition halls is not allowed, neither are baby buggies. Visitors to the Sacred Relics exhibition are requested to wear appropriate clothing; no shorts, mini-skirts or tank tops. There are no guides but an audio guide is available. Admission is free for disabled visitors and one companion although some parts of the museum are not wheelchair accessible. There are cafés, snack bars and gift shops on site.

ASIA

– CHINA –

THE FORBIDDEN CITY (THE PALACE MUSEUM), BEIJING

Located in the heart of Beijing, the Forbidden City was home to China's emperors from the Ming dynasty to the end of the Qing dynasty. Nowadays in China it is more often referred to as the Palace Museum.

The 178-acre walled compound that once shielded emperors and their extensive entourages from public view houses around 1,000 buildings. Ninety of these are palaces and altogether there are more than 8,000 rooms. Many are open to the public.

Back in 1406 construction of the Forbidden City began, with at times more than 100,000 artisans and up to 1 million workers involved. Materials, only the best, included whole logs of wood from the rare Phoebe zhennan tree and huge marble blocks. The size of the workforce meant building the palace was completed in only fourteen years. And you may well ask, why does it have the rather off-putting name, Forbidden City? It was because in the days of the Ming and Qing dynasties ordinary people were forbidden to enter without permission. When building was complete, the Emperor Yongle decided to move the capital of his empire to Beijing, from Nanjing.

The Forbidden City is divided into the Outer Court and the Inner Court. The Outer Court is the southern part and features three main halls; the Hall of Supreme Harmony, Hall of Central Harmony and Hall of Preserving Harmony. The Hall of Supreme Harmony, sometimes called the Hall of Golden Chimes, is the most important and largest structure in the Forbidden City. Built in the 15th century, it was where ceremonial occasions took place – things like the emperor's birthday and coronations. In the middle, there is a spectacular dragon throne which the emperor sat on to preside and while in his presence the entire court would touch the floor nine times with their foreheads in the custom known as 'kowtowing'. At the back of the throne is a carved Xumishan, the Buddhist paradise, signifying the throne's supremacy.

Behind the Hall of Supreme Harmony is the smaller Hall of Central Harmony, which was where the emperor went to make last-minute preparations for state occasions, rehearsing speeches and receiving important ministers. On display are two Qing-dynasty sedan chairs, which were the emperor's mode of transport around the Forbidden City.

世界人民大团

The last of the Qing emperors, Pu Yi, preferred to go by bicycle though, so some parts of the palace grounds were changed to accommodate him and his bike.

The Hall of Preserving Harmony was where banquets were held. At the back of the hall is a 250-tonne marble carriageway embellished with carved dragons and clouds. This was conveyed into Beijing on a temporary road made of ice. In days of yore, the emperor was carried over this scene in his sedan chair as he ascended or descended the terrace. The outer housing surrounding the three great halls was used as a store for carpets, silver and gold.

The Inner Court is the northern part of the Forbidden City and comprises the Palace of Heavenly Purity, where the emperor slept, the Hall of Union, and the bedchamber of the empress which was the Palace of Earthly Tranquillity. Other major buildings in the Inner Court include the Hall for Abstinence, Hall of Sincere Solemnity and Hall of Mental Cultivation. The latter was the emperor's bed chamber and office space in later years. The Inner Court was also where religious ceremonies and administrative activities took place. At the far north end of this Court is the Imperial Garden.

All females who lived in the Forbidden City had to stay in the Inner Court, they weren't allowed to go elsewhere. Besides the royal females, most women were employed as servants, though a favoured group were concubines who had to bear the emperor's children. If they were fortunate enough to have a baby boy, they were promoted to the role of imperial consort.

A 1925 report recorded more than 1,860,000 items left by the Qing imperial family. This astonishing collection included: ancient jade artefacts from the earliest dynasties of Chinese history; paintings, porcelain, enamel and lacquer ware; gold and silver ornaments; bamboo, wood and horn antiques; gold religious statues; thousands of imperial robes; furniture; books and historical documents. Some were displayed to the public, but shortly before the outbreak of the Second World War, the Japanese occupied part of China's north-east and marched on Beijing. The museum authorities packed the treasures into crates and sent them off to Shanghai for safekeeping for the duration of the war.

Interesting facts about the Forbidden City:

• Traditional Chinese colours: white, black, red, yellow and green were used in the palace design.

• The Forbidden City was the home of 24 emperors for 491 years from 1420 to 1911, when the last emperor abdicated. The 1987 film, *The Last Emperor*, was filmed here.

• This UNESCO-listed site is the world's largest palace complex and the world's largest collection of ancient wooden buildings.

Address: The Forbidden City, 4 Jingshan Front St, Dongcheng, Beijing

Website: www.theforbiddencity.org

Visitor Information: According to the China National Tourist Office, the Forbidden City gets on average 15 million annual visitors. The only entry for tourists is through the south gate (Meridian Gate). The main visitor route follows the central axis from the south entrance to the north and takes around two hours. It's easy to spend a whole day here because the area is so vast. Tickets and audio guides are sold on the square before this gate. Over 25 languages are available but some non-native English speakers prefer the English version over their own language because Roger Moore, he of James Bond fame, narrates it.

– INDIA –

MYSORE PALACE, KARNATAKA

Mysore Palace, also known as Ambavilas Palace, is probably the most visited destination in India after the Taj Mahal, attracting around 6 million visitors a year. It is in the centre of the city in the old fort.

It is indeed a beautiful palace, all grey granite and deep pink marble domes, as befits the official residence of the Wadiyar dynasty who ruled the Kingdom of Mysore from 1399 to 1950.

In its lifetime it has been rebuilt several times but the current three-storey palace was constructed between 1897 and 1912. The previous wooden palace was burnt down, so Maharaja Krishnaraja Wadiyar and his mother Kempananjammanni Devi instructed British architect Lord Henry Irwin to build a new one. In the meantime, the family took up residence in nearby Jaganmohan Palace.

Maharaja Jayachamarajendra Wadiyar extended the Palace around 30 years later and added the Durbar Hall wing, a large, pillared communal hall to be used for public announcements and hearings.

For much of their 600-year-old history the Wadiyar dynasty has tried, so far unsuccessfully, to ward off a curse. 'May the Wadiyars of Mysore not have children for eternity,' said Alamelamma, wife of a king whose empire the Wadiyars annexed back in the 1600s. She was cross because in 1612, the then king of Mysore dethroned her husband Sri Rangaraya, governor of Srirangapatna – an adjoining kingdom. She decided to pay them back by stealing the royal ornaments. She might have known she wouldn't get away with it and when they tracked her down she committed suicide to escape arrest. Before killing herself she cursed the royal family.

Perhaps in an effort to counteract the curse, the Wadiyars built a statue of Alamelamma at Mysore palace where she is worshipped as a deity. However, it seems Alamelamma isn't impressed and the curse is still in force.

In 2015 the royal family appointed 22-year-old Yaduveer Chamaraja Wadiyar as new heir to the throne following the death of Srikantadatta Narasimharaja Wadiyar. Yaduveer is not the former king's biological son, but a distant nephew. Srikantadatta and his wife were childless. Since the curse, the Wadiyars have had children only in alternate generations. Whenever a monarch could not have a child, a child was adopted from the extended family. Now that means Yaduveer is 27th king of the erstwhile Kingdom of Mysore.

On 27 June 2016, over a year after his coronation, Yaduveer Wadiyar married Trishikha Kumari, daughter of the Dungarpur royal family from Rajasthan. Both families matched the couple's horoscopes before the marriage and after discussion, decided to go ahead and arrange the nuptials.

Their wedding was an elaborate affair with a vegetarian feast which required more than 200 chefs. On the menu were such delicacies as *kashi halwa* – a traditional sweet;

Photo: Anooperuvessi212

kheer – a kind of rice pudding; *badam kheer* – a creamy dessert made from almonds and milk; *bisi bele bhaat* – a spicy rice dish; *tovve* – a dal vegetable curry; *rasam* – soup traditionally prepared using tamarind juice as a base and *majjige huli* – vegetables in buttermilk.

The couple were an alternate generation and following the pattern since the curse, Yaduveer and Trishikha had a baby boy on 6 December 2017.

Although the royal family still live in part of the palace, much of it is now a museum housing souvenirs, paintings, jewellery and royal costumes once owned by the Wodeyars. One of the major exhibits is the wooden Royal Throne decorated with ivory, gold, silver and jewels, although it can be seen only during the autumn Dasara festival. At other times it is taken apart and stored for safe keeping. Tradition has it that it dates back to the 14th century and was given to Raja Wodeyar who became monarch in 1610. He was the one who inaugurated the Dasara celebrations, a ten-day Hindu festival celebrating the victory of good over evil. During that time the castle is lit with thousands of lights.

Entrance to the palace is via the 'Gombe Thotti' or Dolls Pavilion which, as its name suggests, houses a collection of dolls from the 19th and 20th centuries as well as Indian and European artefacts. However, perhaps the star of the show is a wooden *howdah*, a frame that sits on an elephant's back, to carry its passengers, decorated with over 80 kilos of gold. At the front of the Pavilion are seven canons which are fired to mark the beginning and end of the Dasara procession.

Visitors to the palace can see the Ambavilasa, a luxurious private hall with rosewood carved doorway and a magnificent collection of paintings by top Indian artists. There's also the impressive octagonal Marriage Hall with stained glass ceiling decorated with peacock motifs, originally made in

Glasgow, Scotland. The colourful floor reflects the peacock design with English-made tiles. Another room of the palace well worth seeing is the Armoury, with its arsenal of weapons from the 14th to early 20th centuries.

Interesting facts about Mysore Palace:

• Besides Mysore Palace, there are six more palaces in Mysore:

Jaganmohan Palace was a temporary royal residence during the construction of the current Mysore Palace between 1897 and 1912. It is now an art gallery used by Maharaja Jayachamarajendra Wadiyar.

Jayalakshmi Vilas Palace was the University's administration office and is now a folk art museum.

Rajendra Vilas Palace, once a guest palace for visiting maharajas, is now a private hotel. Similarly the Lalitha Palace, used by British envoys and governors, is now a five-star hotel.

Cheluvamba Vilas Palace is the headquarters of a Food Technological Research organisation while the Krishnarajendra Vilas Palace has become the Krishna Rajendra Hospital.

• Magnificent courtyards and gardens surround the palace while the cellar's labyrinth of tunnels lead to several secret areas and even, it is rumoured, to the nearby town of Srirangapatna.

• A sound and light show takes place at Mysore Palace every day except Sundays and public holidays from 7 pm to 7.45pm, after which the main building is illuminated for a further fifteen minutes.

Address: Mysore Palace, Chamrajpura, Mysuru, Karnataka 570001

Website: http://mysorepalace.gov.in/

Visitor information: The palace is around one mile from the main railway station and six miles from the airport. Entrance to the old fort is free but there is an entrance fee for the palace. Cameras are not allowed but can be held securely at the entrance. There is also a footwear stand and for those with limited mobility, there is a free wheelchair facility. Allow around two hours for the visit.

– JAPAN –

HIMEJI CASTLE, HYŌGO

Nicknamed 'White Heron Castle' or 'White Egret Castle' due to its white colour and bird-like appearance, the castle perched on a hilltop and regarded as Japan's most spectacular complex invites a triple take.

Himeji Castle was originally built in 1346 by Akamatsu Sadanori as a fortification against local shoguns. A UNESCO World Heritage Site, one of the first to be registered in Japan, Himeji is one of only twelve completely original castles in the country. Built on the site of an ancient fort – which in turn was built on the site of a sacred shrine – the six-storey-high castle, an eclectic collection of 83 wooden buildings, is a monument to the Japanese concept of harmony between man and nature.

It was built with a granite base which allows it to sway slightly when earthquakes happen along, while the thick, bullet-resistant plaster on the walls acts as fire-proofing. In fact the castle is in the top league when it comes to defences, with moats, towers, walled alleyways, triangular gun ports and rectangular arrow slits from which defenders could fire their weapons. Gate mechanisms also ensured that stones would be dropped on the enemy if they managed to enter, while floor hatches meant that attackers would get boiling water poured on them – interestingly not the usual boiling oil, because in this castle's case it would have stained the plaster. A kitchen in the inner court meant the occupants wouldn't starve in the event the castle fell under siege. None of these things were ever put to the test though because the castle has never seen combat. It survived air strikes during the Second World War and also came through the Great Hanshin earthquake of 1995 unscathed.

Besides the main complex there are several other buildings, residences and storehouses. They are enclosed by stone walls, the middle and outer moat and connected by corridors and passages.

Otemon Gate is the main gate into the castle, allowing visitors access to the admission-free part, the outer bailey called the San-no-maru. Lawns here are littered with cherry trees and it is a lovely, though busy, place to come for a picnic in cherry blossom season.

Going through the Hishi Gate leads to the part of the castle which requires a ticket. Once inside the main keep, there are six sets of narrow staircases for visitors to climb. They actually get steeper as they approach the top, so be warned! There are no fripperies or furniture inside the castle, no decorations, paintings or statues. That's not how they do things here – the castle displays the austere lifestyle of

Photo: Lukas

its previous inhabitants. There are however plenty of strong doors with big bar locks, giant hooks on the walls to hold weapons and no end of nooks and crannies all designed to confuse any would-be invaders. If you do decide to climb all the way to the top you may be able to see from the windows some of the adornments on the tops of the castle towers. These are *shachi* – make-believe animals with lions' heads and the bodies of fish. You can also access the only one of Himeji's three surviving moats by going through the Hishi Gate. Boat rides are available at weekends.

In 1931 Himeji was designated a 'national treasure'. Restoration work started in 1956 and finished in 1964, then another restoration project began in 2010 and was completed in 2015.

Interesting facts about Himeji Castle:

• It took around 10,000 people to build the castle using pine and granite from nearby mountains.

• The fight scene in James Bond's 1967 *You Only Live Twice* was filmed here.

• The castle's wooden framework comprises huge pillars including an 800-year-old cypress beam. It's supposed to be lucky to touch it.

Address: Himeji Castle, Honmachi 68, Himeji City, Hyōgo Prefecture 670-0012

Website: www.city.himeji.lg.jp/guide/castle_en.html

Visitor information: Castle tours take place several times throughout the day. Steep stairs with narrow treads and uneven paths have to be negotiated, so these may not be suitable for the less mobile visitor. Be aware that you have to remove your shoes before going inside, and mind you don't bump your head on the low doorways if you are tall. If you want something to remember your visit, head for the castle's gift shop.

And, an interesting end note, usually it's only towns that are twinned with each other, but at the time of writing, Conwy Castle in Wales (see page 126) is set to be twinned with Himeji Castle. That's a first for the UK!

– THAILAND –

GRAND PALACE, BANGKOK

Slap bang in the centre of Bangkok, the Grand Palace was the home of the kings of Siam (now Thailand) and seat of government from 1782 for 150 years. It is Thailand's most popular tourist attraction.

The palace, in actual fact a complex of buildings, was last permanently occupied by the royals and government in 1925, before they started to drift away to other locations. All government departments left for the last time in 1932 with the abolition of the absolute monarchy. However, it is still used for official and state functions and the royal family still exists in Thailand, though no longer rules.

The palace has two main sections, Wat Phra Kaew or the Temple of the Emerald Buddha, and the royal residence.

The residence itself has three courts – outer, centre and inner. Visitors arrive at the outer court, where the army and treasury were based, functions over which the king had a direct interest. As far as the Emerald Buddha goes, this miniature statue of Buddha was painstakingly crafted from a single piece of jade – not emerald, as the name might suggest. Don't think you can touch it for good luck though as it sits high above tourists' heads and is kept in a glass box. You can't take a photo of it either. It came here via Vientiane, capital of Laos, by Chao Phraya Chakri who went on to become King Rama I, when he captured the city in 1778.

The Emerald Buddha has three golden costumes, and they are changed seasonally at a ceremony presided over by the king of Thailand. In winter Buddha is dressed in a solid gold robe, in summer he wears a diamond encrusted one and when the rainy season comes it means it is time for his gilded monk's robe.

The temple entrance is guarded by statues of two mythical sixteen-feet-high giants. It's as you'd expect of a temple that is Thailand's most sacred site. What's more, visitors must dress appropriately before being allowed entry. (For details on what is considered appropriate, see visitor information below.)

Exiting the temple leads to the Central Court, where the king held audiences and did his state business. On one side is the Boromphiman Throne Hall, built around 1900 and the most modern building in the palace. Built by King Rama V for his son King Rama VI, its extended front portico is where carriages can stop and visitors alight under cover, though it is not open to the public. Incidentally it was Rama VI who threw his hands up in horror at the tradition of harems. Until he came to the throne, the palace's harem was housed in the Inner Palace area and guarded by female sentries. He obviously thought one wife was sufficient. Good for him.

Next to the palace's newest building is its oldest. The Phra Maha Monthien Palace Group contains the Chakraphat Phiman Hall, main residence of the first three kings of the Chakri dynasty. Then there is the Phaisan Thaksin Hall, a massive room where kings dined and held informal meetings, and the Amarin Winichai Mahaisun Audience Hall which has two thrones – one was later used as an altar. The hall is open to the public but only on weekdays. The Ratcharuedee Pavilion was used for the king's purification (the bath he took during his birthday rites) and was also used on other ceremonial occasions, while the Dusidaphirom Pavilion was a chamber where the king would dress before taking rides on his elephant. The nearby Dusit Maha Prasat Throne Hall dates back to 1790 and today is used for the lying in state of members of the royal family. The hall has a mother-of-pearl throne and a bed which royals used for relaxing between formal occasions.

Interesting facts about the Grand Palace:

• One of the original royal services housed in the outer court was the 'elephant department', charged with taking care of the king's elephants used for war and travelling around the country.

• If you are told by locals and tuk-tuk drivers that the palace is closed, it may well be a scam to get you to visit other places, that they are very happy to sell you tickets for (at extortionate prices). Ignore them and head on to the ticket office to check for yourself.

Photo: Francisco Anzola

- If you have time, visit the nearby Temple of the Reclining Buddha. The temple complex houses the largest collection of Buddha statues in Thailand, including the amazing 46-metre- (150-foot)-long gold-plated reclining Buddha.

Address: Grand Palace, Na Phra Lan Road, Grand Palace, Phranakorn, Bangkok 10200

Website: www.tourismthailand.org/Attraction/The-Grand-Palace--52

Visitor information: The Grand Palace is open every day. To get there take the Chaophraya Express Boat to Chang Pier. Walk through the market around the pier and onto the plaza. The long white palace wall is across the street. You can't really miss it and the entrance is the second gate in the wall. Arrive early because it gets very busy after 9am with tour groups and also gets very hot. You have to remove your shoes before going inside and there are shelves in front where you can leave them. However don't wear your best, most expensive shoes to come unless you have a bag to put them in because some thefts have been reported.

There is a strict dress code for visitors to the Grand Palace. Men must wear long trousers and sleeved shirts, no vests or tank tops. If you're wearing sandals or flip-flops you must bring socks, in other words, no bare feet. Women must be similarly modestly dressed. No see-through clothes, short skirts or shorts or bare shoulders. If you arrive at the front gate improperly dressed, there is a booth near the entry that can provide cover-ups, but you must leave your passport or credit card as security.

AFRICA

– SOUTH AFRICA –

CASTLE OF GOOD HOPE, CAPE TOWN

South Africa's oldest existing colonial construction was built by the Dutch East India Company in the late 17th century. It served as a place of replenishment for ships en route from the Netherlands to the Dutch East Indies, now Indonesia.

The structure built in the mid-1600s replaced an older clay and timber fort, the Fort de Goede Hoop. A bell tower was added in 1684. The original bell, South Africa's oldest, was cast in Amsterdam and its purpose was to announce the time, as well as warning citizens of danger.

Built with the blood, sweat and tears of commandeered soldiers and sailors, women, slaves and members of the traditional nomadic indigenous population the Khoi, who were forced to work as punishment, the castle, a pentagonal stone fortress, was the centre of civilian, political and military life. It housed a bakery, shops, cells and living quarters. Today the castle is the seat of the military in the Cape.

In 1695 a defensive wall called a 'Kat' was built diagonally across the courtyard. This was to protect the fort from a land attack and housed the residences of the governor as well as the second-in-command. There was also a council hall that doubled as a church. The Kat Balcony, the entrance

Photo: Bernard Gagnon

to the governor's residence, has fluted pillars, wrought-iron railings and curved staircases. From this balcony, public announcements and judicial sentences were read.

During the Second Boer War (1899–1902) part of the castle was used as a prison and visitors can still see the cells. There is a double cell where drunken soldiers were kept until they regained their sobriety, while a large two-doored cell held up to twenty prisoners at any one time. It must have been a horribly cramped space to live in. Another double cell was the ablution cell and came with a primitive stone bath. Inscriptions made by prisoners are still visible and there is a story that they used nails from their shoes to carve them. The last time the cells were used was during the Second World War, to detain prisoners from passing ships on their way to the east.

Fritz Joubert Duquesne, the man who killed Lord Kitchener and leader of the Duquesne Spy Ring, was one of the prison's more well-known residents. Although the castle walls were thick, Duquesne was determined to escape and doggedly dug away the cement around the stones with an iron spoon. He nearly succeeded in escaping one night, but a large stone slipped and pinned him in his tunnel. The next morning, a guard found him unconscious but alive.

There is also a chamber – not for the faint-hearted – where prisoners were tortured. The castle was built on the shore line, and so high tides filled its moats. When large waves came along the dungeon would fill with water, and prisoners who were chained to the dungeons walls often drowned. Probably due to the castle's bloody history, it claims to have a phantom or two. Records say one ghost, a tall figure of a man, was seen on the castle's battlements in 1915. The same phantom has been seen several times since then. Who was he in life? No one seems to know.

In 1936 the castle was declared a historical monument and from 1969 it became known as a national monument. Extensive restorations were completed during the 1980s making the castle the best-preserved example of a Dutch East India Company fort.

Today visitors enter the castle through the main gateway, which was built between 1682 and 1684 to replace the original entrance. Remember to look up when entering as the pediment above the entrance has the coat of arms of the United Netherlands. On the architrave below are carved the arms of the Dutch cities of Hoorn, Delft, Amsterdam, Middelburg, Rotterdam and Enkhuizen, cities where the United East India Company had chambers.

Interesting facts about the Castle of Good Hope:

• The castle houses three museums: the military museum; the William Fehr Collection which has fine examples of paintings and antique furniture; and there is the permanent ceramic exhibition, 'Fired', situated in the castle's old granary.

• Clinker bricks, also known as *IJsselsteen* brought as ballasts in Dutch ships, were used as decorative features in parts of the castle.

• Yellow paint was originally chosen for the castle walls because it diminished the effects of the hot African sun.

Address: Castle of Good Hope, Castle and Darling Street, Cape Town, 8001

Website: http://castleofgoodhope.co.za

Visitor information: The castle is in Cape Town's city centre near the central station.

Guided tours operate seven days a week. Visitors can also see the key ceremony which takes place every day. This is where the Van der Stel entrance is unlocked by ceremonial guards, an old established custom. Directly after that, there is a cannon firing ceremony. This originated to indicate that a ship had been sighted at sea and to let those in the fort know. Mind your ears because it is very loud!

An in-house deli serves light bites and drinks.

Visitors can also see a blacksmith in action, just as he would have worked in the 17th and 18th centuries when castles had their own smithy. Climb to the battlements for far-reaching views over Table Mountain, the city and beyond.

NORTH AMERICA

– CANADA –

CRAIGDARROCH CASTLE, VICTORIA, BRITISH COLUMBIA

This Victorian-era Scottish baronial mansion is a designated National Historic Site of Canada. It would be best described as a 'bonanza castle', the name given to mansions built by entrepreneurs who made their fortune during the industrial age, and is probably as close to a European castle as visitors are likely to see in North America.

Thirty-nine-room Craigdarroch was built by Scottish immigrant and coal baron Robert Dunsmuir during the reign of Queen Victoria. He came from a village in Ayrshire and when he was 22 years old married nineteen-year-old Joan White. Eight days later their first child Elizabeth was born. Four years later, in 1851, the family sailed for Canada where Robert had signed on with the Hudson's Bay Company. It was a last-minute decision, taken only after someone else backed out, leaving a space.

In subsequent years Dunsmuir made his fortune from Vancouver Island coal, and in 1887 he commissioned work to start building Craigdarroch as a family home. Unfortunately he died in April 1889, a year before his mansion was completed. His sons Alexander and James completed the construction after his death.

To use a modern-day term, at the time, the family would have been considered 'dysfunctional'. One of the daughters became engaged to a married man with children, another spent much of her life in an insane asylum, while one of the sons was an alcoholic and had a mistress for twenty years who was unwelcome at Craigdarroch because she was divorced.

It was certainly quite an accomplishment that 38 years after arriving in Canada as an indentured $5-a-week miner for the Hudson's Bay Company, Robert Dunsmuir died the richest man in British Columbia in sole control of an empire estimated to be worth $15 million Canadian dollars (around $409 million today). However, part of the reason for Dunsmuir acquiring this hoard of money was that in truth he wasn't a very fair or kind man to do business with or to work for. He employed large numbers of Chinese workers in his mining operations and paid them half of what he paid Caucasian workers. He also paid his employees one third less than his competitors paid their workers.

Photo: Michal Klajban

The building, which has seventeen fireplaces and around 20,000 square feet of interior space, has a magnificent oak spiral staircase and fabulous stained glass throughout. There is a nod to the family's Scottish roots with a bust of Scots novelist Sir Walter Scott and a thistle stained-glass window. From the ballroom on the fourth floor there are wonderful views to the south of the Olympic Mountains. Visitors can also admire the rather grand billiard table in the games room and an extensive collection of leather-bound books in the library where there is a quote from Bacon's essays above the fireplace: 'reading maketh a full man'. If you want to go to the top floor, be prepared to climb 87 steps.

Over the years the castle has had a number of functions including as a college and music school and underwent substantial renovation in 1919 when it became a military hospital. A major refurbishment was carried out in 1979 when it was purchased by the private Craigdarroch Castle Historical Museum Society.

Joan Dunsmuir lived in Craigdarroch until her death in 1908 and there is a story that her ghost now haunts her former home. Visitors and staff have reported seeing objects move and hearing disembodied voices. Some even claim to have taken photographs of Joan and heard her play the piano while yet others have reported smelling her favourite tallow candles in her room. Overactive imaginations? Who knows …

Interesting facts about Craigdarroch Castle:

• In Gaelic, the castle's name means 'a rocky old place'.

• Craigdarroch has been a film location for several films including *Little Women* (1994). Since 2000 it has also housed several theatrical productions including *The Importance of Being Earnest* and *The Fall of The House of Usher.*

• The castle exterior is a combination of marble, granite, sandstone, terracotta and Vermont slate.

Address: Craigdarroch Castle, 1050 Joan Crescent, Victoria, BC V8S 3L5

Website: https://thecastle.ca/

Visitor information: The castle is open daily and audio tours are available. As a historic house museum there are no ramps or lifts and the building is not wheelchair accessible. It is available as a venue for weddings and other events. Visitors have to use an automatic shoe cleaner before entering the castle's main hall to help keep the carpet and floors of this heritage home unsullied.

– UNITED STATES OF AMERICA –

'IOLANI PALACE, HONOLULU, HAWAII

The only royal palace on American soil, dating back to when Hawaii was a kingdom. Built between 1880 and 1882 in a unique style known as 'American Florentine', it was the official residence until 1893 of the last two monarchs, King Kal kaua and his successor and sister Queen Liliuokalani.

Photo: Thomas Tunsch

King Kal kaua was the first monarch to circumnavigate the globe. Well, so they say. Certainly, there are many influences from around the world apparent in 'Iolani's design, especially from the palaces and castles of Europe.

'Iolani Palace was very modern in its time, it even had the first electric lighting and flushing lavatories on the island and there was an internal telephone system too. It certainly put the White House to shame. Queen Liliuokalani didn't have it all though because the US government overthrew the monarchy in 1893 and established an interim administration. Meanwhile the poor Queen was held prisoner in her own home for almost eight months.

In 1898 the Hawaiian Islands became annexed to the USA but it wasn't until 1959 that they became the 50th American state. After annexation the palace was taken over by administrators and became the government's executive offices. Contents were catalogued and those considered unsuitable to the building's new role were sent to auction.

During the Second World War, after the bombing of Pearl Harbour, the palace was used as headquarters for the military. It was also the scene of a mass swearing-in ceremony of Hawaiian soldiers of Japanese descent who formed the 442nd Infantry. However, with all this going on, no one cared much about 'Iolani's historical and architectural importance, and so it became neglected and fell into disrepair.

In the mid-sixties, governor John Burns decided it would be a good idea to launch a campaign to restore the palace to its former glory. It was recognised as a National Historic Landmark in 1962 and in 1968 the administration moved to a new building.

Local research was carried out to identify the palace's original layout, furnishings and how it was used. As a result of this and of course with substantial fundraising, around half of the palace's original furnishings were bought back from private ownership around the world and rooms restored to their original appearance. When all that was finished, the palace was thrown open to the public in a blaze of glory in 1978.

Visitors can retrace the building's history and walk its 7,000 square feet of glorious wooden flooring (wearing cloth booties handed out at the entrance to protect the floors). The Grand Hall runs the length of the palace and has a magnificent staircase made from Hawaiian koa wood. Walls in the hall are hung with royal portraits. The large Throne Room, decorated in regal reds and gold, was the venue for state occasions and magnificent balls. On a sadder occasion though it was also the scene of the queen's trial, that was before she was imprisoned in an upstairs room.

On the opposite side of the hall from the Throne Room is the Blue Room where smaller, less formal functions took place. The State Dining Room's walls are adorned with paintings of European leaders and the Music Room is decorated in golden tones.

The King's Library was his office where he spent much of his time and visitors can see artefacts from the days of his reign. The basement overflows with royal regalia, including swords, jewellery and the king and queen's crowns. It's a nice touch that each year their birthdays are celebrated, the king's on 16 November and the queen's on 28 December.

The land on which the palace sits is believed to have been a place of worship in ancient times. The grounds are accessed by one of four gates, each one displaying the kingdom's coat of arms and visitors can see the coronation pavilion here too, which looks like a traditional bandstand. Another interesting sight is that of the Sacred Mound, burial site of Hawaiian kings and chiefs, but visitors can't get too close thanks to the fence erected to respect those who are buried there.

The 'Iolani barracks were built around 1870 as the headquarters of the Royal Guard. Since the overthrow of the monarchy the barracks have performed a number of functions, including as the headquarters of the national guard and as a club for servicemen. In 1965 the barracks were dismantled and moved to their current location and they now play a new role as palace shop and ticket office.

The palace's vision statement says "Iolani Palace is a living restoration of a proud Hawaiian national identity and is recognised as the spiritual and physical multicultural epicenter of Hawaii, representing the thriving dignity of the unique people of Hawaii.'

Interesting facts about 'Iolani Palace:

• While Queen Liliuokalani was held captive in the palace she made a large patchwork quilt, which is on display in the room she was imprisoned in.

• The coronation pavilion is the location for inauguration ceremonies for the state's governor.

• The Kanaina Building was the first building in the US to be erected for the preservation of public archive materials.

Address: 'Iolani Palace, 364 South King Street, Honolulu, HI 96813, Hawaii

Website: www.iolanipalace.org

Visitor information: 'Iolani Palace is open Monday–Saturday.

Visitors can tour the first and second floors of the palace and there is an audio guide. There are also guided tours every fifteen minutes that need to be booked in advance. Tours in Japanese take place every day at 11.30am and tours in Mandarin and sign language can also be booked. The palace is also used for private events such as weddings. Don't take your camera in though – it is forbidden to take photos inside.

NOTES